D0169939

IMBOLC

LLEWELLYN'S SABBAT ESSENTIALS

IMBOLC

RITUALS, RECIPES & LORE FOR BRIGID'S DAY

Llewellyn Publications
Woodbury, Minnesota

FIRST EDITION
Eleventh Printing, 2021

Book format by Bob Gaul
Cover art by iStockphoto.com/18232461/©Electric_Crayon
 iStockphoto.com/5522170/©artbyjulie
 iStockphoto.com/50512128/©Atypeek
 Shutterstock/234507625/©Valentyna Chukhlyebova
Cover design by Kevin R. Brown
Editing by Laura Graves
Interior illustrations by Mickie Mueller

Llewellyn Publications is a registered trademark of Llewellyn Worldwide Ltd.

Library of Congress Cataloging-in-Publication Data
Neal, Carl F., 1965–
 Imbolc: rituals, recipes & lore for Brigid's Day/Carl F. Neal.—First Edition.
  pages cm.—(Llewellyn's sabbat essentials; #8)
 Includes bibliographical references and index.
 ISBN 978-0-7387-4541-1
1. Saint Brigid's Day. 2. Witchcraft. 3. Neopaganism. I. Title.
 BF1572.S325N43 2015
 299'.94—dc23
                    2015024050

Llewellyn Worldwide Ltd. does not participate in, endorse, or have any authority or responsibility concerning private business transactions between our authors and the public.

 All mail addressed to the author is forwarded but the publisher cannot, unless specifically instructed by the author, give out an address or phone number.

 Any Internet references contained in this work are current at publication time, but the publisher cannot guarantee that a specific location will continue to be maintained. Please refer to the publisher's website for links to authors' websites and other sources.

Llewellyn Publications
A Division of Llewellyn Worldwide Ltd.
2143 Wooddale Drive
Woodbury, MN 55125-2989
www.llewellyn.com

Printed in the United States of America

Contents

...on sleep, cleansing, sprouting seeds, fertility, transitions, protec...

...n, rebirth, transformation, youth, well-being, emergence, awakenin...

...mid midpoint between the winter solstice and the vernal equinox,...

...15 degrees of aquarius in northern hemisphere, sun at 15 degre...

...uthern hemisphere, female: the goddess transforming from crone t...

...e goddess in the form of young mother tending to her growing c...

...t in the form of a child exploring the world, the innocence of th...

...Brigid, Aphrodite, Diana, Arianrhod, Artio, Athena, D...

...Inanna, Juno, Selene, Vesta, Telu, Februus, Braga, Cupid,...

...Cocht, Dumuzi, Eros, light green: abundance, growth fertility,...

...alming, new beginnings and prosperity, pink: harmony, tenderne...

...n, love, spiritual healing, virtue, spring, honor, contentment, white...

...peace, protection, healing, truth, divination, purification, childho...

...vitality creativity, communication, the sun, planning, psychic a...

...angelica: balance, new beginnings, consecration, insight, purificat...

...success, basil: clarity, divination, love, money, protection, streng...

...berry: growth, attachments, fertility, intuition, prosperity, prot...

...mon: balance, blessings, courage, protection, purification, streng...

LLEWELLYN'S SABBAT ESSENTIALS

LLEWELLYN'S SABBAT ESSENTIALS provide instruction and inspiration for honoring each of the modern witch's sabbats. Packed with spells, rituals, meditations, history, lore, invocations, divination, recipes, crafts, and more, each book in this eight-volume series explores both the old and new ways of celebrating the seasonal rites that act as cornerstones in the witch's year.

There are eight sabbats, or holidays, celebrated by Wiccans and many other Neopagans (modern Pagans) today. Together, these eight sacred days make up what's known as the Wheel of the Year, or the sabbat cycle, with each sabbat corresponding to an important turning point in nature's annual journey through the seasons.

Devoting our attention to the Wheel of the Year allows us to better attune ourselves to the energetic cycles of nature and listen to what each season is whispering (or shouting!) to us, rather than working against the natural tides. What better time is there to start new projects than as the earth reawakens after a long winter, and suddenly everything is blooming and growing and shooting up out of the ground again? And what better time to meditate and plan ahead than during the introspective slumber of winter? With Llewellyn's Sabbat Essentials, you'll learn how to focus on the spiritual aspects of the Wheel of the Year, how to move through it and with it in harmony, and how to celebrate your own ongoing growth and achievements. This may be your first book on Wicca, Witchcraft, or Paganism, or your newest addition to a bookcase or e-reader already crammed with magical wisdom. In either case, we hope you will find something of value here to take with you on your journey.

Take a Trip Through the Wheel of the Year

The eight sabbats each mark an important point in nature's annual cycles. They are depicted as eight evenly spaced spokes on a wheel representing the year as a whole; the dates on which they fall are nearly evenly spaced on the calendar, as well.

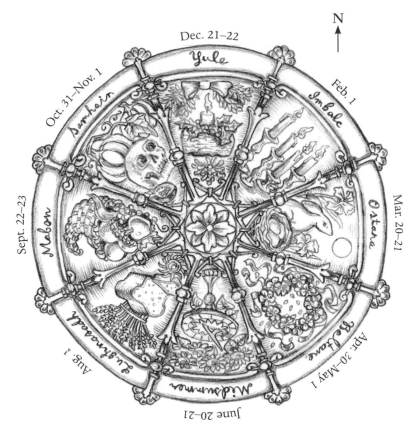

N

Dec. 21–22 — Yule
Oct. 31–Nov. 1 — Samhain
Feb. 1 — Imbolc
Sept. 22–23 — Mabon
Mar. 20–21 — Ostara
Aug. 1 — Lughnasadh
Apr. 30–May 1 — Beltane
June 20–21 — Midsummer

Wheel of the Year—Northern Hemisphere
(All solstice and equinox dates are approximate,
and one should consult an almanac or a calendar
to find the correct dates each year.)

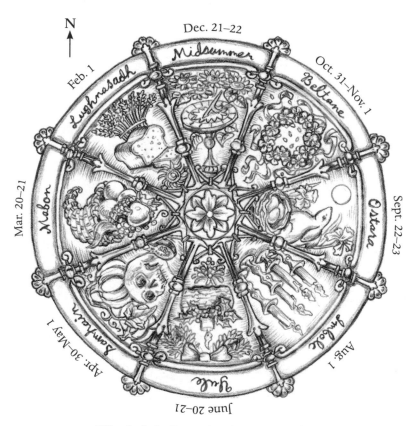

N ↑

Dec. 21–22

Feb. 1

Oct. 31–Nov. 1

Lughnasadh

Midsummer

Beltane

Mar. 20–21

Mabon

Ostara

Sept. 22–23

Apr. 30–May 1

Samhain

Imbolc

Aug. 1

Yule

June 20–21

Wheel of the Year—Southern Hemisphere

The wheel is comprised of two groups of four holidays each. There are four solar festivals relating to the sun's position in the sky, dividing the year into quarters: the Spring Equinox, the Summer Solstice, the Fall Equinox, and the Winter Solstice, all of which are dated astronomically and thus vary slightly from year to year. Falling in between these quarter days are the cross-quarter holidays, or fire festivals: Imbolc, Beltane, Lughnasadh, and Samhain. The quarters are sometimes called the Lesser Sabbats and the cross-quarters the Greater Sabbats, although neither cycle is "superior" to the other. In the Southern Hemisphere seasons are opposite those in the north, and the sabbats are consequently celebrated at different times.

While the book you are holding only focuses on Imbolc, it can be helpful to know how it fits in with the cycle as a whole.

The Winter Solstice, also called Yule or Midwinter, occurs when nighttime has reached its maximum length; after the solstice, the length of the days will begin to increase. Though the cold darkness is upon us, there is a promise of brighter days to come. In Wiccan lore, this is the time when the young solar god is born. In some Neopagan traditions, this is when the Holly King is destined to lose the battle to his lighter aspect, the Oak King. Candles are lit, feasts are enjoyed, and evergreen foliage is brought in the house as a reminder that, despite the harshness of winter, light and life have endured.

At Imbolc (also spelled Imbolg), the ground is just starting to thaw, signaling that it's time to start preparing the fields for the approaching sowing season. We begin to awaken from our months of introspection and start to sort out what we have learned over that time, while also taking the first steps to make plans for our future. Some Wiccans also bless candles at Imbolc, another symbolic way of coaxing along the now perceptibly stronger light.

On the Spring Equinox, also known as Ostara, night and day are again equal in length, and following this, the days will grow longer than the nights. The Spring Equinox is a time of renewal, a time to plant seeds as the earth once again comes to life. We decorate eggs as a symbol of hope, life, and fertility, and we perform rituals to energize ourselves so that we can find the power and passion to live and grow.

In agricultural societies, Beltane marked the start of the summer season. Livestock were led out to graze in abundant pastures and trees burst into beautiful and fragrant blossom. Rituals were performed to protect crops, livestock, and people. Fires were lit and offerings were made in the hopes of gaining divine protection. In Wiccan mythos, the young goddess is impregnated by the young god. We all have something we want to harvest by the end of the year—plans we are determined to realize—and Beltane is a great time to enthusiastically get that process in full swing.

The Summer Solstice is the longest day of the year. It's also called Litha, or Midsummer. Solar energies are at their apex, and the power of Nature is at its height. In Wiccan lore, it's the time when the solar god's power is at its greatest (and so, paradoxically, his power must now start to decrease), as he's impregnated the maiden goddess, who then transforms into the earth mother. In some Neopagan traditions, this is when the Holly King once again battles his lighter aspect, this time vanquishing the Oak King. It's generally a time of great merriment and celebration.

At Lughnasadh, the major harvest of the summer has ripened. Celebrations are held, games are played, gratitude is expressed, and feasts are enjoyed. Also known as Lammas, this is the time we celebrate the first harvest—whether that means the first of our garden crops or the first of our plans that have come to fruition. To celebrate the grain harvest, bread is often baked on this day.

The Autumn Equinox, also called Mabon, marks another important seasonal change and a second harvest. The sun shines equally on both hemispheres, and the lengths of night and day are equal. After this point, the nights will again be longer than the days. In connection with the harvest, the day is celebrated as a festival of sacrifice and of the dying god, and tribute is paid to the sun and the fertile earth.

To the Celtic people, Samhain marked the start of the winter season. It was the time when the livestock was slaughtered and the final harvest was gathered before the inevitable plunge into the depths of winter's darkness. Fires were lit to help wandering spirits on their way, and offerings were given in the names of the gods and the ancestors. Seen as a beginning, Samhain is now often called the Witches' New Year. We honor our ancestors, wind down our activities, and get ready for the months of introspection ahead … and the cycle continues.

The Modern Pagan's Relationship to the Wheel

Modern Pagans take inspiration from many pre-Christian spiritual traditions, exemplified by the Wheel of the Year. The cycle of eight festivals we recognize throughout modern Pagandom today was never celebrated in full by any one particular pre-Christian culture. In the 1940s and 1950s a British man named Gerald Gardner created the new religion of Wicca by drawing on a variety of cultures and traditions, deriving and adapting practices from pre-Christian religion, animistic beliefs, folk magick, and various shamanic disciplines and esoteric orders. He combined multicultural equinox and solstice traditions with Celtic feast days and early European agricultural and pastoral celebrations to create a single model that became the framework for the Wiccan ritual year.

This Wiccan ritual year is popularly followed by Wiccans and witches, as well as many eclectic Pagans of various stripes. Some Pagans only observe half of the sabbats, either the quarters or the cross-quarters. Other Pagans reject the Wheel of the Year altogether and follow a festival calendar based on the culture of whatever specific path they follow rather than a nature-based agrarian cycle. We all have such unique paths in Paganism that it is important not to make any assumptions about another's based on your own; maintaining an open and positive attitude is what makes the Pagan community thrive.

Many Pagans localize the Wheel of the Year to their own environment. Wicca has grown to become a truly global religion, but few of us live in a climate mirroring Wicca's British Isles origins. While traditionally Imbolc is the beginning of the thaw and the awakening of the earth, it is the height of winter in many northern climes. While Lammas may be a grateful celebration of the harvest for some, in areas prone to drought and forest fires it is a dangerous and uncertain time of year.

There are also the two hemispheres to consider. While it's winter in the Northern Hemisphere, it's summer in the Southern Hemisphere. While Pagans in America are celebrating Yule and the Winter Solstice, Pagans in Australia are celebrating Midsummer. The practitioner's own lived experiences are more important than any dogma written in a book when it comes to observing the sabbats.

In that spirit, you may wish to delay or move up celebrations so that the seasonal correspondences better fit your own locale, or you may emphasize different themes for each sabbat as you experience it. This series should make such options easily accessible to you.

No matter what kind of place you live on the globe, be it urban, rural, or suburban, you can adapt sabbat traditions and practices to suit your own life and environment. Nature is all around us; no matter how hard we humans try to insulate ourselves from nature's cycles, these recurring seasonal changes are inescapable. Instead of swimming against the tide, many modern Pagans embrace each season's unique energies, whether dark, light, or in between, and integrate these energies into aspects of our own everyday lives.

Llewellyn's Sabbat Essentials offer all the information you need in order to do just that. Each book will resemble the one you hold in your hands. The first chapter, *Old Ways*, shares the history and lore that have been passed down, from mythology and pre-Christian traditions to any vestiges still seen in modern life. *New Ways* then spins those themes and elements into the manners in which modern Pagans observe and celebrate the sabbat. The next chapter focuses on *Spells and Divination* appropriate to the season or based in folklore, while the following one, *Recipes and Crafts*, offers ideas for decorating your home, hands-on crafts, and recipes that take advantage of seasonal offerings. The chapter on *Invocations and Meditations* provides ready-made calls and prayers you may use in ritual, meditation, or journaling. The *Rituals and Celebrations* chapter provides three complete rituals: one for a solitary, one for two people, and one for a whole group such as a coven, circle, or grove. (Feel free to adapt each or any ritual to your own needs, substituting your own offerings, calls, invocations, magical workings, and so on. When planning a group ritual, try to be conscious of any special needs participants may have. There are many wonderful books available that delve into the fine points of facilitating ritual if you don't have experience in this department.) Finally, in the back of the book you'll find a complete list of correspondences for the holiday, from magical themes to deities to foods, colors, symbols, and more.

By the end of this book you'll have the knowledge and the inspiration to celebrate the sabbat with gusto. By honoring the Wheel of the Year, we reaffirm our connection to nature so that as her endless cycles turn, we're able to go with the flow and enjoy the ride.

OLD WAYS

...m sleep, cleansing, sprouting seeds, fertility, transitions, protec...

..., rebirth, transformation, youth, well-being, emergence, awakening

...nd midpoint between the winter solstice and the vernal equinox,

...5 degrees of aquarius in northern hemisphere, sun at 15 degree...

...thern hemisphere, female; the goddess transforming from crone to...

...goddess in the form of young mother tending to her growing ch...

...in the form of a child exploring the world, the innocence of the...

...Brigid, Aphrodite, Diana, Arianrhod, Artio, Athena, Pa...

...Inanna, Juno, Selene, Vesta, Sela, Februus, Braga, Cupid,

...Eecht, Dumuzi, Eros, light green: abundance, growth, fertility,

...luing, new beginnings and prosperity, pink: harmony, tenderness

...love, spiritual healing, virtue, spring, honor, contentment, white:

...eace, protection, healing, truth, divination, purification, childhoo...

...tality, creativity, communication, the sun, planning, psychic at...

...angelica: balance, new beginnings, consecration, insight, purificati...

...success, basil: clarity, divination, love, money, protection, streng...

...berry: growth, attachments, fertility, intuition, prosperity, prote...

...mon: balance, blessings, courage, protection, purification, strengt...

$\mathcal{W}$HEN THE DARK days of winter seem to have gone on forever, the first sign of spring refreshes our souls. It is a promise that winter will not last forever and that warm and fertile days will come again soon. Even through snow, the daffodils will push their heads up with a startling flash of green and yellow against the otherwise unbroken glare of winter's white. While you can still see your breath like steam in the chilled air, the first taste of fresh milk means that new life will soon be born. Weary from winter's dark, it also means that the soul will soon be reborn in the growing warmth of the sun. There yet may be snow on the ground but there are new plants sprouting just beneath that protective layer. As bears awaken from their winter slumber, so too does the earth, and life everywhere reawakens.

Also known as "Imbolg," "Oimelc," and the "Feast of St. Brigid," Imbolc is the sabbat midway between the winter solstice and the vernal equinox. Imbolc is celebrated on February 1 and precedes the more recent Christian reinterpretation of Imbolc called "Candlemas" which is celebrated on February 2. Although you might often see the terms *Imbolc* and *Candlemas* used interchangeably, they are actually different holidays. Imbolc is the time when life begins to awaken from its winter sleep and prepare for the warmer and longer days that are soon to start. During the depths of winter, it can feel as though the warm sun and soft breezes of spring will never return and the cold might go on forever. Imbolc marks the turning point when life eagerly begins to look forward to the increasingly warmer days.

Imbolc is a time when new plans are made and new ideas are "planted." It is also traditionally a time to examine the people, objects, and philosophies in our lives. It is an opportunity to discard the things we don't need or that are holding us back. It is when we make new plans and improve old ones. In a sense, the Imbolc part of the Wheel of the Year is a winter cocoon. Upon emerging, we may be greatly changed indeed from the beings who celebrated Yule only weeks before.

Winter to the Ancients

Although we all experience winter to some extent regardless of where we live, the way modern civilizations deal with winter makes it a bit more difficult to understand just how important a milestone Imbolc was to many of our ancestors. Although it is true that Imbolc as a sabbat grew from the celebration of the first milk from the pregnant ewes in the hinterlands of Ireland, Scotland, and other parts of Europe, this sabbat is surprisingly relevant to us today as we stay in our safe, warm, climate-controlled homes and automobiles regardless of how savagely the winter rages outside our doors.

To truly understand the roots of Imbolc and why it has been incorporated as a sabbat for modern Wiccans and Neopagans, you have to imagine what life was like in Europe (and many other parts of the world) in antiquity. Even as recently as two hundred years ago, winter was a much different experience than it is today. Now imagine what it was like five thousand years before *that*. Consider that the things we take for granted were completely absent at that time. Food preservation was much more limited and laborious than it is today; canning wasn't developed until the reign of Napoleon in nineteenth-century France. There were no freezers, refrigerators, or vacuum sealers. Forget about plastic containers to store food. There weren't any grocery stores for times when supplies ran low. Our ancestors dealt with challenges that are difficult for us to imagine in the twenty-first century.

The ancients were very clever and intelligent folk who took advantage of snow and cold waters for refrigeration, and they made use of the sun, fire, salt, and fermentation to preserve food for long winters. Challenges were constant, and the hardships they endured are hard to grasp for the modern, convenience-oriented mind. Please note that when you see the term "ancestors" in this book, it doesn't necessarily refer to people with whom you might share a lineage and genetic material. Instead, "ancestors" in this book refers to any ancient peoples, as they are all the ancestors of humankind. Many Neopagans walk spiritual paths with deities who come from a heritage different from their own. While "ancestor worship" generally means worshiping of one's progenitors, you personally might choose to venerate the deities from a completely different culture than the one(s) of your forebears. Indeed, there is some debate in the Neopagan community about the practice of ancestor worship, and those who choose to honor ancestors who are not their own genetic progenitors may have very valid reasons for doing so.

In many parts of the ancient world, staying warm in winter required keeping a large supply of fuel for the fireplace. There were no quick drying clothes made of synthetic fibers or sleeping bags rated for -40°F. The only lighting available came from a flame. How frightening is it to think about living in a wooden building with a thatch roof while using fire as the only source of light and heat? It certainly gave people of the age a healthy respect for fire and its life-changing properties (both positive and negative)! Living so closely with nature in her many forms taught our ancestors to have deep reverence for the animals and plants that surrounded them.

Winter can be dangerous for modern people, but the dangers cannot be compared to what our ancestors faced. You could not call 911 if someone was sick or injured, not to mention there was no fire brigade should one of your flames get out of control. If heavy snows caused your roof to collapse, your entire family could potentially perish from a lack of shelter.

Useful hours of daylight in winter are very limited, and simply completing all the daily chores to maintain life was challenging in the winter for our ancestors. The abundant harvest faded away as winter grew. Certainly dried and salted foods kept people alive during the winter, but often even the best preserved foods would mold, rot, or be eaten by vermin (whose supplies also ran low during the winter). Hunting and/or fishing could provide inconsistent supplemental nourishment, but these practices were never dependable during the dark days of winter.

In agricultural societies, people had to feed their livestock through the winter. Samhain (late October) was usually when the last animals were slaughtered before the cold set in. Animals that were not slaughtered at Samhain had to be cared for throughout the winter along with the people. Without those animals in the spring, the food chain would be broken and starvation could easily follow. Food had to be carefully stored for the animals as well as the humans.

It is difficult for people who live in modern cities to understand the relationship our agrarian ancestors had with their animals. In agricultural societies, people love their animals as much as we care for our pets but in a very different way than we would understand it. They care for their animals as if they were members of the family because they are so integral to life. It was very common in agricultural societies in colder climes for families to bring their animals into the home to live until warmer days arrive.

While I doubt that many modern ranchers in North America or Europe sleep in the same room as their cattle or sheep, historically this was considered prudent and frugal. When you think about how very critical livestock was to survival and add the difficulty of trudging through snow or ice to reach an external barn, sleeping with the animals makes sense. The animals will contribute to the warmth of the home, and having them so close would make feeding and caring for them much easier as well, although this convenience came at the cost of very cramped and uncomfortable living conditions. Needless to say, sanitation was a significant concern as well.

Although spring planting represents an important step in survival, those seeds won't yield food immediately. On the other hand, if you take care of your animals through the winter, they can start producing food for you long before the first plants. Imbolc marked that point in the year for ancient Celtic peoples. Sheep will naturally tend to mate in the autumn as the days begin to grow shorter; they are called "short-day breeders" for this reason.[1] Their gestation period tends to be around five months, so the result is that ewes tend to breed in September to October and begin to give birth around Imbolc.[2] As soon as the ewe gives birth, she is stimulated to begin lactation. In the modern world of sheep production, humans have been able to stimulate breeding whenever it is most convenient for the rancher. In the ancient world, however, the cycle was much more under nature's control. In those old times, the birth of lambs meant the first fresh milk in months. Fresh milk and the resulting cheese were among the first signs that spring was about to arrive. On the Celtic Wheel of the Year, Imbolc represents the beginning of spring.

Can you imagine living such a life? You're trapped inside your single-room home with your spouse, children, and likely your parents, cousins, and in-laws too, plus most of your food and your animals all winter. Is it any wonder that as soon as the first signs of spring appeared that the people would celebrate? After carefully rationing wine or beer for months and drinking melted snow sometimes mixed with a few precious leaves to make an herbal tea, just think how good that first taste of milk would be.

Winters in the Western world can be dangerous no matter how advanced technology might become. The dangers we face are real enough, but our (obviously quite durable) ancestors dealt with risks we don't even have to consider. Even now when severe winter storms hit or there are power failures, we seldom see deaths in our modern cities. Our ancestors had no public transportation, "warming centers," or National Guard to rescue them from the depths of a terrible winter; they survived by their own skills and wits along with a strong connection to their communities, nature, and the deities who steered them through their daily lives.

Even with ample fuel for the hearth, temperatures often dropped miserably low, just as they do now. Remember that not only was infant mortality quite high in the ancient world, Imbolc was a time of childbirth. Babies conceived at Beltane (a frequent occurrence) are born around Imbolc. If disease and lack of food were not enough to make winters risky, the cold itself claimed many infants. How difficult it must have been to keep the family and livestock safe and then have to give birth and care for a newborn child. Is it any wonder our ancestors treated the element of fire with such deep reverence and respect? When we think about all the hardships and challenges our ancestors faced in the winter months, it makes even the thought of the coming spring much brighter and more important.

Ancient Cultures and Nature

In our age of telecommunication and air travel, it can be difficult to see the world as our ancestors did. Many people in the modern world are very isolated from nature and rarely encounter it on its own terms. Our forebears were more attuned to nature because they lived in it. "Nature" as a separate concept would be difficult for them to grasp; they were part of nature's fabric. It's a far cry from the many people today who only encounter nature on certain cable television channels.

As discussed on the previous pages, winter's difficulties in earlier times often led to death. While many like to think that we have bested nature or have command over it in the twenty-first century, humans in earlier times had no illusions about their place in nature. It may be hard for us to imagine, but not so long ago a harsh winter could quite literally bring wolves to your door. Humans were not at the top of the food chain, and winter was the most dangerous time of all. Knowing when winter would pass and when to expect the first new plants and melting snow meant more than knowing when to plant. It meant knowing a brighter future lay ahead if the hard winter could be endured. Then, as now, knowledge is power… and power brings the mind comfort.

Every spring celebration could be seen as a celebration of surviving winter more than anything else. Our ancestors observed animals and animal behavior as closely as we might watch a modern weather forecast. In many ancient cultures, animals figured into predicting weather and seasonal phenomena.

Celtic

The modern calendar recognizes the vernal equinox, or Ostara, as the beginning of spring. In the Celtic calendar, Imbolc represents the start of spring. Animals could be put out to pasture and were no longer dependent on stored hay. Barns and homes that had been shuttered throughout the long winter could be cleaned or at the very least aired out. There were newly born animals in the pens which also meant a fresh flow of milk. In many ways, this point on the calendar represented a time of cleansing, renewal, and rebirth.

Brigid

It is simply impossible to talk about Imbolc without talking about the very powerful Celtic goddess Brigid. She is also called "Brighid," "Brigit," "Bride," and "Brigantia," among other names, but is mostly widely known among Wiccans and Neopagans as Brigid. She is a goddess of many forms and has presented herself as all three aspects (maiden, mother, and crone) of the Earth Goddess. Over many generations, she has proven to be not only powerful, but also a very durable goddess. Although most closely associated with Ireland (she is often called the Goddess of Ireland), Brigid was also an important goddess in Scotland, Wales, and many parts of Western Europe.

Brigid is a goddess of fire and flame, change, poetry and inspiration, transformation, wisdom, metalworking and the fire of the forge, healing, creativity, water, prophecy, education, and learning. She is credited with giving the written word to humanity. Brigid is also a goddess of childbirth, and she can be called upon for help during delivery to keep mother and child safe. In many places it was a tradition on Imbolc to open all of the doors and windows in the home and for the women of the house to stand at the threshold in order to receive Brigid's blessings.

Called the Goddess of the Eternal Flame, Brigid is charged with its protection; her shrine in Kildare, Ireland, held the Eternal Flame, where it was guarded night and day. It is said that for its safety, the sacred flame was surrounded by a hedge that no man could penetrate; only Brigid and her priestesses could pass through it. As a goddess of fire, Brigid is often called upon to protect homes from its destructive power. Brigid's Crosses and corn dollies are often hung in kitchens to entice her protection over hearth and home. She is also called the "Great Teacher," and might have been one of the earliest advocates for womens' education.

Brigid is also called the Goddess of the Sacred Well; in this capacity, she protects its healing waters. While some say the well was also hers to protect within the shrine at Kildare, others point to her sacred well at Liscannor in County Clare, Ireland, instead. In fact, the utter domination of Brigid and her shrines and legions of followers resulted in the area around Kildare often being called the "City of Brigid."

She is credited with creation of the whistle as a defensive weapon against attacks on women.[3] A powerful shapeshifter, Brigid can appear in almost any form: she may appear as a woman of any age in her aspects as maiden, mother, and crone; a bird; smoke or a pillar of fire; or even a woman with a flaming head. She has also been said to transform into a snake and is sometimes represented in that guise in various works of art.[4] She is simultaneously a mother, wife, and daughter to the Celtic gods, displaying another sacred triple aspect.

Given that Brigid is a goddess of fire, it is not surprising that she is also a goddess of change and transformation, ideas the Celts considered to be represented by fire. Just as a forest is transformed after a wildfire, so too are we transformed after being touched by Brigid's transforming fire. Relatedly, as the Goddess of the Forge her fire is used to reshape and refine the rocks of the earth into forms that serve humanity. Simple ores are combined and catalyzed within her flame, the result of which are materials totally new and different, such as steel or bronze.

Brigid is a central figure in Celtic mythology and the embodiment of the triple goddess. According to the mythos, there are actually three sisters all named Brigid. One is Goddess of the Hearth Fire, one is Goddess of the Forge Fire, and the third is Goddess of the Creative/Transforming Fire. The three Brigids were forged together into one triple-aspected goddess (notice again the trinity, as three is a sacred number).

The common theme throughout the stories and poems of the Celts—and seen in this short overview of this goddess— is that Brigid is all about transformation and new beginnings, just like Imbolc. This is a sabbat that is about preparing for what is to come, getting rid of old things that no longer serve us, and introspection. Imbolc is about beginnings and the transformation from winter to spring.

Saint Brigid

If you have any doubt about Brigid's ability to transform herself, you need only look at her fate after the Christian suppression of the Celts' native religions. Even after Christianity's arrival in Ireland, the cult of Brigid was simply too strong for proselytizing Christians to dismiss. If Christianity was to take hold in Ireland, the goddess Brigid had to be included. In so many instances when Christianity displaced local deities, the latter were often relegated to being characters in fairy tales, completely forgotten, or even transformed into demons or monsters. No such fate would befall the Goddess of the Eternal Flame, however. Instead, we find the sudden (and virtually inexplicable) appearance of Saint Brigid. Although no longer described as a "goddess," her credentials as a saint were undeniable.

St. Brigid was put forth as the midwife to Mary when Jesus was born. That reconstructed history provided a clever way for the Church to let her keep her deep connections with childbirth. In other stories, Saint Brigid healed lepers using the water from her well, and she blessed the baby Jesus with three (there's that trinity again) drops of water on his head. This part of the saint's history redefines Brigid's connection with water in a Christian context. She was also said to bring "bright weather" with her, thus maintaining her connection to spring and the end of winter.

Finally, it was said that St. Brigid was born on February 1 (sometimes called Candlemas Eve). Some stories say that she was born at dawn in a pillar of fire. Others say that her mother gave birth to her at dawn as her mother crossed the threshold into her home. All of these stories put a strong emphasis on symbols of change. Places and times of transition were sacred to Celtic peoples, representing the mystical places that exist only within margins. Dawn, fire, and thresholds are all symbols of change, so St. Brigid was also given a birth that had no deep meaning within Christian tradition but would clearly speak to the Celts the Church wanted to convert. Each of these Christianizations of established Pagan belief made it a little easier to get people to convert. Think about it: if all of your deities and celebrations were part of this new religion but with different names, becoming Christian would be an easier choice.

The shrine at Kildare became a Christian shrine dedicated to St. Brigid. It was said that dead birds were brought back to life at the shrine as one of St. Brigid's miracles. (It would indeed be miraculous to see birds that had not only been killed, but actually cooked and eaten, brought back to life by the healing powers of St. Brigid!) Her "Daughters of the Flame" maintained the perpetual flame in Kildare from the fifth century BCE to the sixteenth century CE under the reign of Henry VIII, when the site was declared Pagan and dismantled.[5]

The creation of St. Brigid wasn't enough to stop the goddess Brigid either. There has been a resurgence of interest in Brigid's pre-Christian form as you will see in the next chapter. St. Brigid also made the journey to the Caribbean with indentured Irish and Scottish servants. There she transformed yet again to become Madame Brigitte in Voodoo belief.

Although the sabbat of Imbolc is based primarily on Celtic practices throughout the British Isles and Europe, this time of year was a time of celebration for many ancient cultures, not only the Celts. Fertility and change are at the heart of many such festivities.

One practice among the ancient Celts was the creation of corn dollies. Now in the US, "corn" refers to maize. In Europe, however, the word "corn" describes any kind of silage fed to livestock. If you're American, to get what you call "corn" in a London restaurant you should order "sweet corn." Otherwise your server will be very confused—but entertained. So when we talk about corn dollies, you should not think of dolls only made of maize (although you certainly could make a corn dolly from maize) but rather a figure made from reeds, grass, or other plant material. In fact, wheat is a very common material used in making corn dollies.

Corn dollies are used to represent the Crone aspect of Brigid when made during harvest (most traditionally at Lugnasadh) but the same type of corn dolly made at Imbolc represent Brigid's Maiden form. Sometimes corn dollies made at Lugnasadh are stored through the winter and brought out again at Imbolc as a symbol of the transformation from Crone to Maiden.[5] At Imbolc the corn dolly (called "the biddy") was placed in a specially made small-scale bed ("Brid's bed") along with a symbol of male fertility such as a wand or stick. The bed was placed in the ashes of the home's hearth fire, sometimes accompanied by burning candles. If the ashes were disturbed in the morning, it was seen as a very positive omen for the coming year.

Roman

Imbolc is certainly not the only ritual holiday during this time of year, nor is it the only one focused on welcoming spring or celebrating renewal and purification as the new season of growth begins. One of the most ancient known celebrations during February was the Roman festival "Februalia" (from which the month takes its name). Februalia was a ritual of purification that took place at the end of the Roman year. This festival offered a chance to honor the gods and the dead, and for people to purify themselves in preparation for the coming year. As you can see, purification is a common theme for rituals and celebrations at this time of the year.

Februalia celebrated the goddess Juno, who shares many qualities with Brigid. The similarities between this Roman celebration and Imbolc made it easy to blur the lines between them. Just as Candlemas replaced Imbolc, so did the Feast of the Purification of the Virgin Mary replace Februalia.

A much better known Roman celebration is "Lupercalia," variously cited as beginning on February 13 or on the last full moon of the Roman year. Lupercalia is generally believed to have supplanted Februalia (which is older), but Lupercalia's focus is distinct despite having inherited traditions from its predecessor. While purification and cleansing remain part of the focus, powerful sexual energies are part of Lupercalia. The central ritual took place at the foot of the hill where Romulus and Remus, the legendary founders of Rome, were suckled by a she-wolf in a cave called *Lupercal*.

This fertility ritual is believed to predate the rise of the Roman Empire, so it is really more correct to label this as an Etruscan ritual. Of course, the Romans were experts at appropriating and incorporating many diverse beliefs into the empire's rituals and beliefs. They certainly embraced the celebration and worked to make it part of their culture for generations. In fact, the ritual continued to be celebrated in Rome until 494 CE, when a Christian feast was declared on that day.

Lupercalia celebrates the god Faunus and goddess Juno. The worship of both of these deities significantly predates the Roman Empire and some of that ancient energy can be felt in the primal nature of this holiday. Faunus is a wild spirit who embodies primitive sexual drive. A horned god, he bestows the ability to see the future or psychic abilities. He does so in ways that often seem frightening, such as nightmares. Faunus is sometimes confused with Pan because their physical appearances can be very similar.

Juno is an ancient goddess of time. She is the protector of women, making her a good counterbalance to the unchecked sexual energy of Faunus. Being a protector of women at all ages,

31

Juno is also the goddess of fertility and birth. She is a healer, but her work is focused on women's health issues only. Juno has existed in different aspects in different times. As Juno Februa, she was directly tied to the Februalia ritual.

The ritual celebration of Lupercalia included sacrifices to the deities. Afterwards, strips of the hides of the sacrificed were cut and given to naked or loincloth-bearing young men. They then ran throughout the ritual area using the strips of hide as whips to strike people. This was a rite performed as a fertility blessing, and many young ladies beckoned and even lined up so they'd be sure to be found and hit with the whip. The belief was that if they received lashes, doing so would increase fertility and ease the pain of childbirth.

Native American

Many Native American tribes traditionally celebrated the Imbolc season, although similar to Chinese New Year, celebrations were more often based on the lunar calendar rather than the solar. Many Native traditions hold that the winter is a mystical time of year. It is when most ceremonies were held, along with feasts, and was seen as a time of transitions and change. Names were given, initiations held, alliances renewed, marriages blessed, and more.

Living in close harmony with nature means that winter is usually seen as part of life and its challenges are simply part of life's beauty. From the Seneca in New York to the Kwakiutl on the Pacific coast and the many tribes in between, numerous Native American peoples have shown a greater embrace of winter's hard facts than some Europeans, who tend to see winter as something to be endured with no merit of its own.

Egypt

An ancient Egyptian goddess similar in many ways to Brigid is also celebrated during the transition from winter to spring. Renenutet is a goddess of protection and childbirth. She is often depicted as a horned or fire-breathing cobra or a woman with a snake's head. She is called upon during labor, and afterward she offers protection to the child. She especially favors premature or sick infants. It is also said that she helps nursing mothers by making their infants want to feed. That in turn helps them to grow and remain healthy.

Renenutet is also a goddess of grain and is celebrated with offerings of milk, bread, and wine, like Brigid.[6] She was celebrated during the transition periods of ancient Egypt's three seasons, all of which revolved around the Nile and its flooding cycle: Akhet, the Inundation (when the Nile's water level began to rise); Peret, the Growth period; and Shemu, the Harvest. The festivals dedicated to Renenutet's celebration at these times of seasonal change might seem very familiar to those who followed Brigid.

Asia

Although we call it "Chinese New Year," this is actually an ancient celebration welcoming spring, marking the start of a new year, very much like Imbolc. The date of Chinese New Year is based on the very old Chinese lunar calendar, so the date can vary anywhere from January 21 to February 19, as it is the second new moon after the winter solstice.[7] *Chun jie* (literally "spring festival"), as it is called in Mandarin Chinese, is actually a two-week-long festival to usher in the New Year, beginning with New Year's Eve—the last night of the last month in the Chinese lunar year—and ending with the the Lantern Festival, which occurs on the fifteenth day of the first month. Imbolc almost always falls on one of those celebration days.[8]

Modern Chinese New Year celebrations are not very different from ancient ones. A dragon or lion marches and dances in celebration, as it was once believed that the loud music accompanying the dance as well as the beast's fearsome gaze would frighten away evil spirits. The dragon a symbol of good fortune (fortune everyone hopes will be bestowed upon them as well) and is also the creature in more than one Asian mythos who turns the wheel of the year. When the wheel completes a full cycle, the dragon returns to start another year for everyone.[9] Firecrackers are used to drive away unwanted spirits, and offerings are made to ancestors and gods for a successful year ahead. Incense is often burned in large quantities to ward off bad energies and encourage good ones. This is also a time of divination and ritual healing, and it is common for people to visit fortune tellers to see what the new year will bring. Although many Asian countries are undergoing rapid growth and modernization, it is comforting to see that this ancient tradition is still being handed down to new generations who continue to practice the tradition with glee.

NEW WAYS

...on sleep, cleansing, sprouting seeds, fertility, transitions, prote...
...n, rebirth, transformation, youth, well-being, emergence, awakenin...
...mid midpoint between the winter solstice and the vernal equinox...
...15 degrees of aquarius in northern hemisphere, sun at 15 degre...
...thern hemisphere, female; the goddess transforming from crone ...
...e goddess in the form of young mother tending to her growing c...
...b en the form of a child exploring the world, the innocence of th...
...Brigid, Aphrodite, Diana, Brigantia, Artio, Athena, V...
...Inanna, Juno, Selene, Vesta, Velu, Februus, Brage, Cupid...
...Cocidi, Dumuzi, Eros, light green: abundance, growth, fertility...
...olming, new beginnings and prosperity, pink: harmony, tenderne...
...n, love, spiritual healing, virtue, spring, honor, contentment, whit...
...peace, protection, healing, truth, divination, purification, childbi...
...uitality creativity, communication, the sun, planning, psychic a...
...angelica: balance, new beginnings, consecration, insight, purifica...
...success, basil, clarity, divination, love, money, protection, streng...
...herry: growth, attachments, fertility, intuition, prosperity, prote...
...mon: balance, blessings, courage, protection, purification, streng...

*I*MBOLC IS THE light at the end of the tunnel, the birth of the new spring. It is a small light, like a candle seen in the distance, because spring is still some distance away. It makes it only right to celebrate Imbolc with candles rather than torches or the blazing balefires that will mark our summer celebrations. To modern Wiccans and Neopagans, all sabbats are celebrations of the element of fire as we acknowledge and celebrate the sun's movement through the skies, marking the changing seasons.

In some ways you could call Imbolc a "sleepy" sabbat—hardly surprising for a sabbat that marks the midpoint between Yule at the depths of the year's dark days and the Vernal Equinox that marks the turn to the light days. Some sabbats like Beltane, Samhain, and Yule are widely celebrated. For many people, Imbolc celebrations may be nothing more than posting "Happy Imbolc" to friends on social media. Although this sabbat is easily overlooked in our modern culture where we can more easily relate to our electronic gadgets than to the rhythms of nature, Imbolc's subtle celebrations can be the harbingers of a wonderful spring and summer to come.

While there are some public rituals and celebrations at Imbolc, the very nature of this sabbat tends to keep the celebrations more private and family-focused than many of the other sabbats. There are several reasons for this; probably the most important one is that this truly is a sleepy sabbat in its own way. As you saw in the last chapter, in ancient times Imbolc was a reason to celebrate because it finally revealed hope for easier days around the corner. It was a sleepy time of the year in a time when travel and communal activities were more difficult. Imbolc celebrations are usually limited to family, although in modern times, families often include people who are not genetically or legally related.

Another reason might be that Imbolc is a very introspective and reflective time. It is a time for self-contemplation and planning. These are quiet, internal activities and in that light you might view Imbolc as a very personal sabbat. It is a time to discard the things that aren't working and plan for new alternatives. Imbolc's very personal nature makes this a more subtle sabbat than some.

One problem some people encounter when attempting to relate to this sabbat is that traditional celebrations don't seem to apply their local geographic conditions. After all, this sabbat is really based on the seasons and climate of northern Europe. Some Neopagans have gone so far as to declare Imbolc to be irrelevant to their practices. And yes, relating to this sabbat might be an issue in some climes if you try to celebrate the preparation of the fields for planting when there are three feet of snow on the ground and the first thaw is still months away.

There are several ways to deal with the apparent disconnect between the sabbat's purpose and your own circumstances come February 1. One way some Neopagans do this is by adjusting the dates of the sabbat's celebration. If you usually see the first flowers of the year in late March you could adjust the date for your Imbolc celebration until that time. Doing so would allow you to keep your spiritual practices in alignment with nature. The various spells and invocations commonly used at Imbolc will seem more applicable since they will reflect what you are actually seeing outdoors. Many Wiccans and Neopagans choose a nature-based spiritual path because it helps them feel more in tune with the planet's rhythms. If that's true for you, adjusting the date you celebrate Imbolc might be the better solution.

On the other hand, if you consider Imbolc the midpoint between the winter solstice and spring equinox, it is difficult to justify celebrating it what may be weeks later. Some Wiccans and Neopagans see things from this heliocentric perspective and don't agree with the concept of "moving" a sabbat. From their perspective, sabbats happen based on where the sun is in the sky and nothing else. If you identify more with this perspective, there are still a few ways to make Imbolc more relevant to you.

In its modern form, Imbolc is often celebrated with a focus on the sabbat's symbolic aspects rather than nature's more physical signs. When you think about the symbols of Imbolc as being mere reflections of the deeper concepts wrapped within the sabbat, it no longer matters if there is snow, rain, or sunshine outdoors. It is easier to identify with the concepts of Imbolc—rebirth, new beginnings, emergence, discarding what is harmful or not needed—when you see those symbols everywhere you go, and those signs in the physical world are merely reflections of greater truths. Just as it is possible to celebrate Samhain regardless of the temperature outdoors, the meanings within Imbolc can be celebrated no matter what you see outside your window.

Celebrating Imbolc at the same time as our ancient ancestors gives us a unique connection to our past and a time when life was much more difficult. This idea has led many Neopagans to paths that make every effort to reconstruct religions predating Christianity and its holidays. There might be several feet of snow on the ground, or your garden may have burst into bloom in January, but either way, performing rituals based on what we know of those ancient ancestors creates new connections to our ancient past. Performing those rituals on the same days those ancient ancestors performed their rituals makes that connection even deeper and more meaningful for many people.

Although visiting Ireland during Imbolc would certainly bring many of the sabbat's symbols to life before your eyes, you don't need to go that far to feel the energies and learn the lessons of Imbolc (or any other sabbat, for that matter). While many Neopagans and Wiccans consider themselves worshipers of the earth, we can learn lessons from every sabbat no matter the weather or temperature. Those challenges might be given to us so we have a chance to learn that sabbats are more than skin-deep with meanings that will resonate regardless of the goings-on of the physical world. Adapting to this and learning to step beyond the expectations of other people's ideas in order to find your own way might be the most important lesson of all.

You don't have to do anything elaborate to connect personally to Imbolc, even in our concrete-reinforced modern world. For example, you could take a walk in the park. While it's not something most of us think about in the early February cold we often have at Imbolc, you may be surprised at how many symbols of the season you can find in many parks and sometimes even in your own yard. Whether the ground is covered with snow or just brown from the dark days, look for the signs of life breaking through. The tiny plants pushing through the snow or the ones fighting the brown landscape with the first signs of a green spring can be found even in the most urbanized areas. Those first plants and flowers are not only the promise for the new start that begins at Imbolc but also proof of how resilient life is.

No matter the problems that might have plagued us in the last year, the time for new beginnings appears in many forms in the world around us if we but take time to look. If you are a gardener (or hope to become one), this is the perfect time of year to choose what plants you are going to grow later. It may be time to buy seed. All those activities help to connect us to nature and her cycles no matter where we live or how disconnected our natural environment seems from our daily lives. Spend an hour at a local greenhouse and soak in the scents of new life and the energy of plants ready to emerge after the cold days.

Brigid in Modern Times

For Wiccans in particular, Imbolc is often a celebration of the goddess Brigid. Many identify this sabbat so strongly with her that they actually call the sabbat "Brigid" rather than Imbolc. For many practitioners, Imbolc is a very personal and meaningful sabbat that remains quite relevant to modern practitioners, and Brigid is at the heart of the sabbat.

Just as she was a central deity to the ancient Celts (and arguably others), Brigid is a key aspect of the face of the universal Goddess. Brigid is the primary or "patron" goddess for many Wiccans and other Neopagans. Among ancient deities still venerated today, Brigid is an unusually good survivor: she made the amazing transformation from goddess to saint, and her popularity survives into our modern era where so many other ancient deities have been lost. More amazing still is her rise in the modern era; not many goddesses become saints and then reclaim their goddess status, but Brigid has done just that!

When the Neopagan movement was gathering momentum in the 1960s, one large sector of the movement used Pagan ideas and deities to demonstrate the strength and post-war empowerment of women. Brigid is a strong, wise, clever, and powerful goddess, and she spoke to many Neopagans and Wiccans as the movement began to grow. Brigid truly represents the potential for any woman to be independent and self-sufficient while retaining her feminine qualities. Brigid shows that women, like men, can accomplish whatever they set their minds to do. Brigid also freed many women from the constraints placed on them by a male-dominated society. Brigid empowers women and men alike to find compassion and inner strength.

The image of a strong goddess is still intimidating to some even in the modern era, but that hasn't slowed Brigid's remarkable comeback as a Pagan goddess. Ironically the Catholic Church's decision to make Brigid a saint was almost certainly a factor in her resurgence as a goddess. Her lore and legend as a saint only grew and kept her alive in the minds and spiritual practices of women until she began to rise again in her full glory as a goddess for a new millennium. In one form or another, Brigid has been worshipped continuously since prehistory.

If you think about it, this resurgence of Brigid is a beautiful representation of Imbolc. Brigid is a goddess known for her effective use of disguise. Although she had beginnings as a Celtic goddess, we could say that she took the guise of a Christian saint out of necessity. The period of her sainthood was not Brigid's true face; it was more of a quieted, resting Brigid, although she continued to help those who called upon her. Then, as if emerging from a cocoon after a thousand-year metamorphasis, she transformed to her proper form as a goddess, completing the circle. And Imbolc is that moment of transformation—it is the moment your decision is made and the changes you desire can begin moving forward. Being introduced to Brigid was that moment of transformation for many women during the early years of Neopaganism.

There are still groups who claim a direct lineage to the original temple and sacred flame. In the twenty-first century there are growing numbers of new organizations of flame keepers and well watchers who serve Brigid, such as the Brigidine Sisters, Solas Beride, and Ord Brighideach, to name a few. There are public organizations dedicated to Brigid as well as secret orders where people serve Brigid much as our ancestors did, despite their living in a technologically advanced society where we have less and less direct contact with nature in every successive generation. Brigid's story is truly one of success, and her worshipers uphold her known traditions with grace.

Dedicants to Brigid follow very traditional approaches to the keeping of the sacred flame in addition to some decidedly modern approaches as well. There are Pagan as well as Christian orders that hold gatherings in person and perform rituals and rites to protect the perpetual flame maintained in their temple or sacred places. There are also keepers who have developed modern magical rituals and spiritual techniques that allow them to accept keepers from around the globe to watch over the sacred flame in shifts.

In what some believe is a modern accommodation to inclusiveness and others think is a return to traditional practices, there are now orders of flame keepers who welcome initiates of any gender. In many sectors of the Neopagan community, being a keeper of the sacred flame was seen as a role for women exclusively. While there are valid reasons for some groups to limit their membership in many different ways, this rigid idea has found flexibility. As Neopagans continue to discuss and address challenges relating to gender inclusion (and even the very concept of gender itself), opportunities are created for everyone. Imbolc is where the seeds of such inclusiveness are planted.

Other Celebrations

Groundhog Day

An annual tradition many of us might consider "purely American" is in reality (like so many other things) a practice deeply rooted in history. In some such traditions, weather forecasting is based on an animal seeing its shadow. Shadows are often powerful magical objects and are sometimes considered entities unto themselves. In the US, it has been an annual tradition for more than a hundred years that every February 2, a hapless ground-hog becomes the center of grand celebrations in Punxsutawney, Pennsylvania. Should the groundhog (in Pennsylvania or any-where else, supposedly) see its shadow as it would on a clear, sunny day, then according to the tradition, there are still six more weeks of winter weather.

The tradition of using the groundhog might have come from early New England farmers who reminded themselves that re-gardless of the weather on that day, they shouldn't have used more than half of the hay they had stored to feed their animals until the new growth of spring ("Groundhog day, half your hay"). While the adaptation of the groundhog to this task likely *is* Amer-ican, the rest of this form of Imbolc divination has its roots thou-sands of years in the past.

Cultures throughout Europe and the Middle East have watched animals on this day as a weather predictor. There is a poem in honor of watching a serpent emerge from the ground on Imbolc, and it seems that Scottish highlanders would pound on the ground in an effort to bring serpents to the surface on Imbolc.[10] Clear, sunny weather at Imbolc meant that more harsh weather was still to come while, ironically, gray and foggy days or those with rain or snow at Imbolc meant that winter has nearly ended. In some traditions it is merely the emergence of a particular animal that is a signal of the spring weather to come.

While this day can be a festive one for many people, it gained some popularity some years ago when a popular movie was made based on this "American" holiday, Actor Bill Murray found himself repeating the same day over and over until he changed himself and his choices in life. Since Imbolc is the time when change begins and when the old is swept away and new ideas and paths are formed, *Groundhog Day* is a very sabbat-appropriate film for Imbolc!

Valentine's Day

February 14 is the feast day of Saint Valentine in the Catholic Church, but in the last century this celebration has been "borrowed" by corporations and transformed into the candy and greeting card holiday we all know (but may not love). In our modern lives, Valentine's Day is about romance and love, especially new love. The origins of our modern celebrations actually extend back to the ancient Roman Lupercalia (discussed in more depth in the "Old Ways" chapter). As it was a mid-February fertility ritual, modern Wiccans might view Lupercalia as a blending of Imbolc (new beginnings) and Beltane (fertility). Remember that the idea of spring beginning on the vernal equinox is a very modern one. Until very recently, many Western European traditions held that spring began at Imbolc instead. You can often see threads of fertility magic (more often associated with the sabbat Beltane) in the lore and traditions of Imbolc.

Interestingly, St. Valentine was purportedly martyred at the command of the emperor Claudius II during the festival of Lupercalia. Thus February 14 was named as the feast of the unfortunate saint. St. Valentine's Day didn't become a day of warning about the excesses of Pagan celebrations of love and love making, as you might think. Instead, St. Valentine's Day took on many of the traditions and symbols of the very Pagan festival that was said to have resulted in the saint's death. And today the process has come full circle, in a sense: the Christian aspects of this celebration added by the story of St. Valentine have all but vanished in the traditions of this "new" holiday, which is now about honoring love and fertility. While now it is more common to receive a gift of chocolates and champagne or flowers than to be flogged with strips of bloody animal hides, our modern celebration of Valentine's Day clearly has more to do with Roman ideas of sex and love than with the martyrdom of a Catholic saint.

Fertility is key in the beliefs of many agrarian communities, and many of its disparate concepts seem to come together starting at Imbolc. While the holiday may get its name from the birth of the first lambs and the first sheep's milk of the year, Imbolc's slightly warmer days stimulate mating in many animals who have shorter gestation periods but still raise their young in the spring , like most birds. That type of primal, mating energy extends far back in the most primitive parts of our collective unconscious. It is unusual that sexual energies and birthing energies exist side by side, but that's definitely the case at Imbolc. We celebrate the coming of the warmer, easier days but also feel the draw of that powerful sexual energy pre-Christian Romans celebrated at Lupercalia.

As Wiccans, Witches, and other Neopagans begin to reclaim the ancient celebrations (rather than the later ones designed to displace them), Imbolc, the Festival of Lupercalia (sometimes incorrectly called the "Festival of Pan"), and other ancient celebrations of the turning of the wheel, we are able to strip away layers of imposed tradition designed to obscure the original celebrations of earth and Goddess.

Mardi Gras

By some definitions, Mardi Gras is a religious holiday, but it is unlikely that many in the Christian Church would agree. Mardi Gras ("Fat Tuesday") is the day before the first day of the Christian season of Lent, which is six Sundays from the Christian holiday Easter. Lent is a time of quiet reflection, fasting, and sacrifice, and it begins on "Ash Wednesday," where the faithful receive an ash cross or smudge on their foreheads. Mardi Gras, therefore, is a holiday that has become a bit of a celebration of the many vices that can be given up for the duration of Lent.

Typified by the celebrations in New Orleans, Louisiana, in the southern United States, Mardi Gras is known for its wild parties involving revelry and sexual energies very similar to the festival of Lupercalia. As mentioned, Lent's beginning is based on the date of Easter, itself based on the lunar calendar, so the date of Mardi Gras can fall within days of Imbolc, although it can also occur as late as early March.

While probably not based on sound Christian theology, the concept of Mardi Gras does fit with Imbolc in its own way. Mardi Gras is a celebration of life and its possibilities. It is a celebration of joy and pure revelry in an effort to clear away that energy to make room for something new. Mardi Gras is a form of spiritual house cleaning for many of its celebrants, just as Imbolc is for Neopagans.

Things You Can Do Today

In addition to the many ancient and modern traditions honoring Imbolc, there are plenty of things you can do without any need for complex rituals or specialized magic tools. Remember that the key element of Imbolc is the emergence from the darkness in preparation for the coming spring. Imbolc is the perfect time to create new plans and make new connections, and prepare for the dramatic change in weather that's on the way. It is also the perfect time to remove obstacles and clear out the energies standing in the way of your life's blossoming spring.

Cleaning

There is no reason to wait for the vernal equinox to start on a good cleaning of spaces that have become cluttered with the trappings of the long winter. While in some regions you may not be able to put your snow boots away quite yet, you can still clean out clutter both physical and magical. Even the happiest homes can become cluttered with the day-to-day, accidental accumulation of objects like magazines, unopened mail, books that were never replaced on the shelf, etc., in addition to the perhaps more subtle accumulation of negative energy from such sources as unexpected bills, arguments about curfews, and other sources of stress in our daily lives. We have more opportunity to air out our homes in warm weather so they are less cluttered in many ways. Months of closed doors can leave layers of unwanted energy, and cluttered spaces can actually cause physical stress in some people.

The act of cleaning a single space in your home can bring in a breath of positive energy that will bring peace of mind and soul. Sometimes cleaning is contagious and others will even join in. If you work hard to avoid physical clutter even in the depths of winter, you can still benefit by clearing away the negative energies that accumulate. You can use a besom (a traditional type of broom used by many Witches, Wiccans, and others) to sweep away negative energy just as you would sweep away dust, but you don't need that specialized tool; an ordinary broom works just as well. It's really wonderful to start by dusting near the ceiling and then working down towards the floor. As you work, visualize all of those accumulated energies clinging to the dust. And when you sweep away the dust, the negative energy goes with it.

Remember that you can help cleanse the spaces of others as well. Service to others has been and still is a part of many Neopagan paths since their beginnings. There are those who are not as able to step up and cleanse a space as easily as most of us. What better way to celebrate Imbolc than helping those who are more physically limited clean their homes? The benefits of cleaning a space of physical and magical "clutter" are amplified for those who are physically limited and rarely spend time anywhere else. You can help others prepare for the coming spring while cleansing your mind and spirit. It only takes the willpower to do it.

Plant a Seed

Although Imbolc falls before outdoor planting is safe in many parts of the world, in the British Isles this sabbat marked the start of spring, and planting was often possible around this time for the ancient Celts. In the modern era we can plant seeds at Imbolc regardless of the temperature outdoors. The seed is both a literal and symbolic representation of Imbolc. Literally the seed represents the beginning of work and the life and nourishment that will result from it; food is the difference between life and death for us all. However, the seed also serves as a symbolic representation of Imbolc because it represents potential. Much like an unhatched egg (often associated with the next sabbat, Ostara), the unplanted, unsprouted seed can hold many things.

While you can look at a seed and often know which species of plant produced it, it's still difficult to tell exactly what you will get if you plant that seed. The seed might sprout and grow into a large, healthy plant, but it could also be weak and barely grow no matter how much care and nurturing you provide. Sometimes a seed doesn't even sprout the kind of plant you expect. You can't tell by looking at a tomato seed if it will make large, hearty tomatoes or if it will produce bushels of cherry tomatoes. Many species of melons produce seeds that are virtually indistinguishable to those of us without a degree in botany. You might think you are planting zucchini but actually have pumpkin seeds. And some seeds never sprout at all. When you look at that humble seed, think about how much potential is there.

Our day-to-day lives are filled with seeds, too. Every project you start, from opening a new business to volunteering at a local festival, is like planting a seed. When you look at a new project, you think you know what it is and what will result. Once you plant it, however, it will grow as nature wishes, and you may end up with something quite different from what you first imagined. Some of the things that grow from these seeds are like annual plants. You do the project once, and as soon as it is concluded you never try that project again. Some of your projects might be "self-seeding," so when one project has been completed it immediately plants the seeds for another to replace it, such as working on an annual fundraiser from year to year.

The most important seeds we plant are with those we love. Once those seeds sprout they are part of your life forever after. Entering into marriage is planting such a seed. Although sometimes marriages die, just as often they grow stronger every year of your life. Children are the ultimate seeds. Once a child has "sprouted" you will tend and nurture it with the expectation that your child will outlive you by many decades. All analogies have their limits, but reflecting on the sprouting and growth from a seed is an idea that can generate many hours of interesting thoughts.

You can manifest this meditation by actually planting seeds, even in the coldest climates. Your local feed store or home store is likely to sell not only seeds but trays, pots, and soil that will allow you to plant indoors even when there is a thick blanket of snow on the ground. If you are a gardener, Imbolc is often a great time to start seedlings indoors to later transplant into your garden when warmer weather arrives. In some climates the soil is warm enough that you can actually plant seeds directly into the ground at Imbolc.

While is easier for gardeners to buy plants ready to go into the ground instead of growing from seed, there is a unique pleasure in growing a plant from seed to full maturity. If you wish to plant seeds as part of this meditation and you already possess a green thumb, simply incorporate this practice into your annual planting.

If you have no plant growing experience or if you've become convinced that you have a brown thumb, you should select seeds that are easy to work with and sprout reliably. Sunflowers are generally easy to germinate and grow, so those might be a good choice. If you are planting outdoors at Imbolc, you could plant radishes or lettuce. Both are pretty forgiving to new gardeners, and radishes will finish growing in just a few weeks. You can also simply meditate on the ideas and concepts around seeds without planting anything.

Whether you plant actual seeds or merely plant seeds in your imagination, the ideas that go along with the seed physically and symbolically are worthy of study and meditation. If you plan to do actual planting, gather your materials at a place where you can work while you sit comfortably. If you plant only in your imagination, try to maintain the same pace that actual planting would require. The best way to accomplish that is to perform every action in your imagination that you would do in the physical world. It may be easier to accomplish that by physically planting a single seed into soil. That one representative seed that you plant might surprise you and grow into a magnificent plant.

Begin by preparing your seedling trays or pots for planting. You may also use soil pellets that expand when wet to become a tiny, biodegradable pot for seedlings. No matter which tools you choose to use, as you prepare the soil for planting, think about the importance of this preparation. Seeds have a chance to grow on any piece of soil where they land if moisture is available, but they will thrive if soil is provided that is loose, moist, and loaded with nutrients. This is especially true if the soil is free of competing plants and water and sunlight are present.

How does this relate to your plans for the coming warm days? If you have any metaphorical seeds—plans or projects, including even old ones coming back to life in the coming year—have you prepared the soil for those seeds to thrive? What can you do to prepare for the planting of your seeds to help ensure they grow to be healthy and strong?

Translating those ideas into the physical world should lead you to question whether you are prepared to carry out the plans held within your seeds. If you are planning to start a new business, have you crafted a business plan or gathered the resources your business will require to operate? Do you have appropriately talented people lined up to handle the work your business will do? Are there any permits or licenses needed for your business? These are all steps that you could take to help prepare the "soil" for the planting of the seed of your new business. You can see that this approach can be adapted to any kind of seed that you hope to grow. Use this meditation to consider what each seed needs before planting begins.

Next, you should plant your seeds. Place the seeds onto or within the soil you have prepared for them. Different types of seeds require different types of planting. Some plants produce small seeds that are scattered on the top of moist soil while others need to be buried an inch below the surface of the soil so that when it awakens it will push its head through the soil's surface on its own. If you are planting unfamiliar seeds, consult the package to ensure you are planting the seeds using the preferred approach.

Now reflect on how those same ideas translate to your upcoming plans and projects. Do you know the best method for planting each of your seeds? If so, are you able to plant your seeds using the best methods? Using the new business example, you might ask yourself if you are locating this business in the best possible place. After all, the physical location of a business can have a significant impact on its success. Are you locating the business in an environment where it will thrive or have you chosen a place that will ensure the seedling will die?

Next, water your newly planted seeds. Different seeds might require different amounts of water to ensure germination. Too much water can wash away tiny seeds, while large seeds might need a deep soaking to become wet enough to trigger germination. Once the seeds sprout, if you don't water the seedlings enough they will desiccate and die. If you water them too much they might die from root rot or from fungus. You have to know exactly how much water to give them for maximum growth. When the time comes, you will have to decide what type of fertilizer to use and how best to apply it to help your new plants to grow.

How do these aspects apply to your physical world projects and plans? Using the new business example, water could be seen as your investment in the company and fertilizer seen as marketing. For different kinds of projects these ideas would still apply, but your task is to try to decide how. What is the water needed for the seeds that you hope to see sprouted by spring?

It seems so simple, putting a dry little seed into some moist soil, but it can be a truly complex metaphor for the plans we make. Imbolc is a time not only to make plans, but to plant the seeds of your plans and ideas into fertile soil so they can sprout and take root in preparation for the growing season that is ready to begin.

Do Something Positive but Out of Character

Imbolc is not only about emerging from hibernation; it is also about making plans for the future. While it is sometimes the wisest decision to continue with our plans from the previous year, Imbolc is a time to review those plans and make changes as needed. While "staying the course" like this can be a good decision, it is also very easy to fall into habits this way. As you examine your plans for the coming year make sure you remain open to new ideas and different approaches. One great way to do that is to use Imbolc as your time to do something you have never done before.

Doing one new thing can easily inspire you to see things in a new light. You might think of it as a cleaning for your brain instead of your home. New activities require us to think in ways we haven't before, possibly giving us new insights into old problems in many aspects of life. You could do something dramatic like flying in an airplane for the first time or running your first 5k, and both would certainly open your mind to new ideas. For most of us, a much smaller step will work just as well. You could do something as simple as going to a movie by yourself for the first time or going to a new restaurant. Talk to a stranger in the line at the grocery store. Try a type of pasta you've never tasted. It's surprising how addictive this can become. If you love art museums, perhaps an afternoon at the roller derby would give you a whole new outlook on your future plans. Use Imbolc to act out of character and do something you weren't sure you could ever do. It can give you confidence to make bigger changes and open pathways to new ways of thinking.

Thank A Deserving Stranger

Imbolc is a transformative sabbat, which is why there is focus on considering new ideas and freeing yourself from old ideas that hold you back. While some might describe this as stepping outside of your "comfort zone," the concept is that speaking to someone that you may only know by sight or a person whose discussions with you have always been "just business" *is* doing something new. You may be anxious about speaking to this person, but even if the encounter lasts only a moment you will feel the energy of taking a step down a new path. There's also the possibility that a positive, new friendship will emerge.

Is there someone at your local library who always finds the book you need? Perhaps there is a clerk at your grocery store who always makes sure your carton of eggs has a rubber band to make sure it's secured. What about the person at work who always holds the elevator door for people who are running just a moment late? We all know someone who has a "thankless" job. Even if they are only the tiniest of things, recognizing the good deeds done by others builds positive energy for you both, and it gives you the benefit of trying something new as well as the satisfaction of recognizing a deserving person. You might also help clear some of the other person's mental clutter from the winter.

Candle-Burning Etiquette

As this is a sabbat very much related to the candle, it is important to understand a few general guidelines for handling candles. Your tradition or path may teach specific guidelines about candles. If so, you should always follow those rules. Otherwise, keep a few things in mind when using them. Candles are often used to light other candles. When doing this you should take care to minimize wax from one candle mixing with the wax of others (especially when they are different colors or created with different energies). The mixing of different candle waxes can be a fun and useful magic technique, but only when done intentionally. Candles are obviously impacted by breezes and should be protected from them as much as possible.

Many Wiccans and Neopagans consider it the height of disrespect to blow a candle out, as the act is seen as using the element of air to defeat the element of fire. To avoid showing such disrespect it is generally considered proper to extinguish candles either by pinching the wick or using a candle snuffer. If you do choose to blow out any of the candles you use for magick, at least take care not to blow any hot wax around while extinguishing the candle. Candle snuffers are inexpensive and come in nearly as many sizes and designs as candles themselves.

SPELLS
AND
DIVINATION

...m sleep, cleansing, sprouting seeds, fertility, transitions, protec...

... rebirth, transformation, youth, well-being, emergence, awakening...

...nal midpoint between the winter solstice and the vernal equinox, ...

...5 degrees of aquarius in northern hemisphere, sun at 15 degree...

...thern hemisphere, female; the goddess transforming from crone to...

...goddess in the form of young mother tending to her growing ch...

...en in the form of a child exploring the world, the innocence of the...

...Brigid, Aphrodite, Diana, Arianrhod, Artio, Athena, Da...

...Inanna, Juno, Selene, Vesta, Sela, Februus, Bragi, Cupid, ...

...Cocht, Dumuzi, Eros, light green: abundance, growth fertility, ...

...lming, new beginnings and prosperity, pink: harmony, tendernes...

...love, spiritual healing, virtue, spring, honor, contentment, white...

...eace, protection, healing, truth, divination, purification, childhoo...

...vitality, creativity, communication, the sun, planning, psychic ac...

...angelica: balance, new beginnings, consecration, insight, purificat...

...uccess, basil: clarity, divination, love, money, protection, streng...

...erry: growth, attachments fertility, intuition, prosperity, prote...

...mon: balance, blessings, courage, protection, purification, strength...

*W*HILE VIRTUALLY ANY magickal working can be attempted at any time of year, spellwork is often enhanced when performed during the special times, such as sabbats, that are most closely related to the work being done. The spells and divinations in this chapter should be adjusted to fit your own needs and the symbols of your particular path. Although Imbolc is strongly influenced by its Celtic roots, there are also workings that come from modern traditions built on beliefs from around the world.

Brigid Candle Divination

Here is a very simple exercise in divination using the emblem of Imbolc: the candle. If you have no experience with divination, this simple technique is a great introduction to this art. You can think of it as being the divination equivalent of a multiple choice question, or almost as a simplified Ouija board.

You will need:

- A small white taper candle *(not a "dripless" candle—a small birthday cake candle will work well for this exercise)*

- A piece of white card stock or thick paper (a white index card is a good choice)

- A permanent marker or ink pen

- A heat and fireproof surface (like concrete, brick, or ceramic tile—you could even use an old ceramic plate)

- A question to ask and possible answers

- A lighter or matches

As is often the case with divination, the most difficult part is creating the perfect question. Make certain your question is specific and clearly defined. A question like "What's the weather going to be like tomorrow?" is not as clearly defined as "Will it rain tomorrow?" Creating the answers to the first question would be difficult because there are so many possibilities.

Write the possible answers to your question on your card stock or paper and mark off a section of the paper for each answer. Observing how the wax melts onto the card will determine which answer is indicated. It is easiest if you plan to ask a "yes" or "no" question, although you could provide many more possible answers. Try to have no more than four possible answers to make interpretation easier.

Using the marker, create one section on your paper for each possible answer. You want each section to be equal in size and all connected in the center. If you are asking a "yes" or "no" question, this could be a simple as marking a single line down the center of the paper and writing "yes" on one side of the line and "no" on the other. If you have four possible answers, divide the paper by marking a cross in the center and writing one answer in each of the quarters created by your marks. The question does not need to be written on the paper, so you can reuse those papers if the same answers will apply to other questions as well.

When selecting possible answers, keep in mind that the answer to your question might not be one of the choices you have listed. If that's a possibility then make one of the possible answers "something else" or "other" to allow for those answers you didn't consider. When you have all of the answers marked in equally sized areas you should attach the candle to the paper or card. The simplest way to do that is to put one or two drops of melted wax (from the bottom of your divination candle or from a different candle) onto the exact center and quickly push the base of the candle into the melted wax. Wait a few moments for the wax to cool, and it will have "glued" your candle to the card.

Your divination candle is ready to use. Place it on a fireproof surface and sit or stand facing it. Make certain that the space you are using has no drafts that might blow the flame around and change the results of the divination. Relax and clear your mind, then very clearly offer your carefully worded question. Begin by calling to Brigid:

Goddess Brigid, Goddess of Flame, Healer, and Keeper of the Sacred Well, I ask that you honor me with your presence today and show me the answer to my question.

Read or state your question aloud, then light the candle. Use matches or a lighter rather than a second candle (which might drip wax and skew the results).

As the candle burns, focus your attention on the candle's flame, watching as it dances and jumps. As you watch the flame, think about your question. Try to visualize it in your mind's eye. Slowly drop your gaze to the candle. Watch as the wax begins to drip down the sides of the candle. Sometimes the wax runs down one side of the candle and continues on that line the entire time it burns but at other times it can take unexpected turns. Because of this, you should allow the candle to completely burn out. Until the candle has burned out, the results from the wax may not be accurate. If you absolutely must extinguish the candle before it burns out, leave it in place and relight it as soon as possible. Never leave a candle burning unattended.

Take care not to let it burn the card stock or paper. If the paper starts to scorch you should extinguish the candle immediately. Otherwise allow it to go out on its own. Once the candle is out, allow it to rest for a bit to cool. If there is a "nub" of candle left on the card, gently rotate and remove it if you can do so without disturbing any of the rest of the wax.

With the wax cooled and "nub" removed (if possible), you can read and interpret the results. Most of the time you will be able to clearly see which one of the answers on your card is covered with the most wax, indicating that answer is the correct one. At other times the wax may flow and pool onto many different parts of the card. The answer with the most wax is the one you should go with. If it is too difficult to determine which has the most wax, you can use a sharp knife to divide the melted wax along the lines between the possible answers. Then peel the wax from the card and compare it (or even weigh it). When it is difficult to decide between two answers with similar amounts of wax, it could be an indicator that there is truth in both of those answers.

Empowerment of the Milk Moon

Sometimes called the Nursing Moon, the Milk Moon is usually the second moon cycle of the Gregorian year and is almost always the moon in the sky during Imbolc. It is the solar calendar that gives us our sabbats but it is the lunar calendar that gives us celebrations based on the cycles of the moon. While these two

71
......

different calendar systems have no mathematical relationship to each other, both systems recognize the realities of life at any given time. As a result, the workings of the two calendars often complement one another., which is definitely the case with the Milk Moon and Imbolc.

The Milk Moon cycle can start as early as December 25 (at the new moon) and end as late as February 22 (dark of the moon). This moon is very applicable to Imbolc, and while there are many wonderful ways to apply the lessons of this lunar cycle, the following spell focuses on self-empowerment. For more ways to apply the moon cycles to your life, I suggest reading a copy of Annette Hinshaw's wonderful book, *Earth Time, Moon Time* (Llewellyn, 1999). Although this spell is best done under the power of the full Milk Moon, it can be performed at any time during this moon cycle.

This working is really for the "givers" in the Wiccan and Neopagan communities, those people we know who are ready to help anyone at a moment's notice. They're the kind of people who will pull over to help a stranger with a broken-down car or offer to help someone move without being asked. They have very generous hearts but often forget this critical bit of logic: if you don't care for yourself, you can't possibly help others. It is one of the first things students learn in any kind of life saving training. Many of the giving types in our communities sometimes are so focused on others that they forget to look inside and care for themselves to ensure they have the strength to help. At times, the giving nature of some people also leads them to be victims of those who would exploit it.

This spell is intended to help with the problem by giving permission to the caster—for *you*—to look within and start healing the hidden wounds of your inner self. Balancing the desire to help others while giving yourself the attention and energy *you* need to have a fulfilling life is difficult. It is not only okay to worry about yourself at times, it is critical for a good, balanced, life.

All you need for this spell is a white candle dedicated to this work and nothing else in a holder, a safe place to set the candle while it is burning, and a view of the moon (looking through a window is fine). As with many spells, it is best to do this working at night, as the moon is not bound by the solar cycles of night and day. Sometimes you'll see a beautiful moon hanging on one horizon and the sun on the other, so the spell might have to be performed in the day. If you are working indoors in that case, try to darken the room as much as possible and cover the window except for an opening where you can clearly see the moon.

Optimally, you should place the candle somewhere it can safely burn *and* where you can sit with a view of the candle and the moon at the same time. If that isn't possible, try to position the candle so it can be easily reached while seated and the moon and candle are visible without having to turn your head too far. Before lighting the candle, sit down and observe the moon. Just look at the surface and allow her energy to penetrate you. The closer the moon is to full, the more energy you will likely feel, but even a crescent moon is powerful. Let your gaze drift over the surface of the moon and quiet your mind. Reflect for a few moments on the intense tranquility you can feel from the moon's energy.

Once you feel settled and quieted, raise your arms to the moon and say:

> *Beautiful Sister Moon—during this cycle of*
> *the Milk Moon, I ask you to nourish me*
> *and help me replenish my own energy.*
>
> *Help me have the things I need in order to help others,*
> *and show me when it would be better to not help.*
>
> *Give me the wisdom to know when to say "no"*
> *and the courage to stand by that decision.*
>
> *As I light this candle, I ask that you send me your*
> *nourishment that even my invisible wounds will heal.*
>
> *Bring your energy to this candle, lit in your honor.*

Light the candle. If you can safely hold the candle, take it with both hands and align it so that the flame appears in the center of the moon as you look at it. Bow in respect to the moon and then place your candle back on a safe surface. Sit quietly and watch the candle burn. As you watch it, think of the things you do for others. Don't think just about the times you did something spectacular, like changing a tire for someone, but also all the little things you do, like holding doors for people, allowing someone to go ahead of you in line at the bank, holding back traffic with your car while a mother duck waddled across the road with her ducklings behind her, and all the ways you give your energy to others; these are all things you have done which are worthy of remembering.

As you watch the moon's power surrounded by your candle's flame, visualize tiny drops of water streaming out of the candle's flame and penetrating deep within you. Each drop helps heal and re-energize you from the inside out, giving you the strength you need to continue helping others.

You shouldn't use this spell as an excuse to sing your own praises to the world. This is a very private undertaking to help your energy reserves grow, not your ego. You may have wounds from helping others and not even realize how past events may be keeping you from doing what you want to do, even if the two are completely unrelated. As you watch the candle burn you should also listen carefully to see if you are given any insight into a particular situation or person.

When you are finished, you should extinguish the flame appropriately. Any time you feel that your energy is depleted by your work for others, light the candle and reflect on your own needs. And remember: don't stop at reflection! When this spell helps you realize a need you have, don't ignore it. Instead, act to address your need so you will be ready to help the next person who needs you.

Blessing of the Candles

With the deep connection between Imbolc and candles, this is also a traditional time to bless candles that will be used throughout the year. If you make your own, you can empower them throughout the candle making process, and it is quite powerful to perform a blessing over all of the candles once they are completed. While the magickal energies of a candle should be aligned as the candle is made, a blessing won't have any effect on those alignments. As a result, you can bless many different types of candles created for any variety of purposes. Healing candles, prosperity candles, and protection candles (or any other variety) can all be blessed together. It is no harm to bless a candle more than once, so if you blessed a candle last year, it is fine to bless it again if it is still unused.

Start by draping your altar or a small table with a white cloth. The colors of the candles won't matter, but you can think of the white altar cloth as being a "blank" color that won't influence the specific energies of the candles you're blessing. For this spell you will not need to walk behind the altar, so you can even use a table against a wall. Place a single white candle in an appropriate holder in the center of the altar. The candle need not be a new one; it is the only candle that will actually be lit as part of the spell and would typically be the only candle on the table that has been previously used.

All styles of candles can be blessed in this way, so gather all the candles you wish to bless. Arrange all of your tapers, pillars, tea lights, votives, candles in containers, and floating candles on your altar in a way that is pleasing to your eye. If any are boxed or wrapped, remove the candles from the wrapping so they can be clearly seen. If you have candles wrapped in clear plastic you can leave it in place. The important thing is that you be able to see each candle.

Stand before your altar and take several deep breaths. Clear your mind as you ground and center. If you are not familiar with grounding, just place your feet on the floor at shoulder width. Raise your arms and breathe slowly and deeply. Visualize roots growing out of your feet and into the floor. The roots rapidly grow into the earth no matter how many floors above the ground you stand. Next, visualize your outstretched arms growing branches extending toward the sky until you are absolutely connected to the air itself. When you can clearly see these things in your mind's eye, you are ready to begin. The deities listed in this spell are all associated with the season of Imbolc but you can (and should) adjust the list to include any patron deities you may have. Also take this spell as an opportunity to reflect on your own practices and pantheon. If you wish to include Ganesha in the list of god aspects you should offer that invocation before the goddess invocation.

Begin with an invocation to the female divine:

*Gracious Goddess, I come before you on this
night/day to ask that your blessings be bestowed upon
these tools of fire and light that I have gathered here.*

*Brigid, Diana, Aphrodite, Danu, and Innana: I call to you,
Goddess, in all your forms to bestow your blessings on these
candles that they always provide the pure and true energy of
the universe while never causing harm or ill to anyone.*

*May these candles always please you
and call you back to their tiny flames.*

Light the white candle you placed in the center of the altar, then offer an invocation to the male divine:

*Great God, I stand before this altar and ask that your blessings
also be given to the candles gathered here tonight/today.*

*Pan, Februus, Bragi, and Cupid, I call to you
in all of your forms to bestow your blessings on
these tools of fire and air that they may always
provide energy that is steady, true, and positive.*

I ask that you guard these candles from
outside energies that might taint them.

May these candles always please you
and call you back to their tiny flames.

Turn your eyes toward the burning white candle. Feel all the energy you have gathered in the space around your altar. As you watch the flame dancing around the candle's wick, visualize that energy coalescing around the flame of the candle. Once the energy is gathered, it will begin to spread out from the candle flame to the other candles on your altar. Visualize the energy reaching out from the candle flame to the wicks of all of the other candles on the altar. The energy may appear as sparks of light that float to the other candles, flashes like tiny lightning bolts, streaks of light that stretch all the way from the flame to the other candles, or in any variety of ways. Just ensure that your visualization includes every single candle (preferably at the wick). That is why it is so important for you to be able to see every candle.

When each candle has been touched by the energy, thank the powers you called:

Great Goddess, in all of your forms you bring blessings
to me every day of my life so I thank you for coming here
to offer the additional blessings upon these candles.

Great God, all of your facets protect me just as you have given protection to the candles gathered here.

Thank you for bringing your energy to me today/tonight.

You should thank any patron deities by name if you called them by name in the first invocation. Your candles can be stowed away until needed. Once candles have been blessed, most people prefer to place them where they are unlikely to be handled by others, especially strangers in your home. This could be accomplished by putting them out of sight in a cabinet or closet but you could even put them on display as long as they are unlikely to be touched, such as inside a china cabinet, on a high shelf, or similar.

Goddess in the Air Divination

Divination is often an art requiring us to interpret symbols. Possible futures aren't usually clearly revealed. Instead we are given signs and symbols that need to be recognized and then interpreted. That is why those who perform divination for others often spend decades learning their craft. Sometimes, however, there are divination techniques that are essentially intuitive to humans. Some forms of divination take advantage of our inborn ability to make symbols more understandable. This is one approach to divination completely tied to personal interpretations and our deepest intuition.

This divination is best performed on Imbolc as we look into the coming warm season, but it could be done on other days as well. It can be done indoors or out. If you decide to do it outdoors you will use clouds as a divination tool, so you need favorable weather. Clear skies won't reveal much to you, nor will a sky completely filled with clouds. Any significant rain or snow will also make it essentially impossible to see any clouds open to interpretation. An alternative and more dependable option is to do this divination indoors using smoke from incense rather than clouds. Interpretation of clouds in the sky or indoors smoke streams are practically the same; the choice of indoors or out is up to you and the weather.

Whatever version of this divination you decide to do, find paper and a pen or pencil.

If doing this divination indoors you will need:

- A censer (burner). *If using stick or cone incense, you may need two censers*

- 2 sticks or cones of incense OR incense charcoal and loose incense or incense pellets

- White tea light candle and holder

- Black (altar) cloth

- A writing utensil and paper or a journal

This divination requires you to be able to see signs in smoke, so it is easy to get carried away and use more incense than needed. It is best done in a room with at least one window. Regardless of the weather, you should open the windows in the room at least a tiny bit. This exercise should only be performed in rooms with good ventilation anyway, and the smoke needs to have access to the outside air so that its energies can escape the room and move out into the universe. And because you need to be able to see the smoke, you will need to create a bit more of it than is normally desired in a spell. If you are using stick or cone incense, you will need two pieces of incense separated by at least four inches to create proper smoke. If you have a censer large enough to accommodate both pieces of incense while keeping them far enough apart you can use it. Otherwise you will need two different censers spaced apart. You could use one stick and one cone if you like. If using charcoal, be certain to light it ten minutes before beginning the divination. Incense blends with a lot of resins will generate the most smoke from the charcoal. Also, the self-lighting variety of incense charcoal burns very hot so it is best to locate higher quality, scentless incense charcoal. If you have to use the self-lighting variety, the high temperature will mean that you have to add more incense to the charcoal frequently. Keep that in mind before you start and make certain you have plenty of incense on hand to feed the hot charcoal.

Indoors or out, you need to be comfortably seated or reclined. With that in mind, if you are working indoors, spread the black cloth on a table or other location that is easy to reach from your comfortable seat. Some people are fine sitting on the floor for this divination, but for most of us a chair and table are the best approach. Also make sure your writing instrument and paper are nearby. Place the censer(s) in the center of the cloth and then place the candleholder three to four inches in front of the censer. If you are using two censers, ensure that they are four inches apart. You can put the candle between the two censers if you would like. Begin by offering an invocation as you light the candle:

Goddess of the Flame, I call upon you and ask that you help reveal to me the Goddess in the Smoke and illuminate the signs she sends to me so that I will see them all.

If you are using incense sticks or cones, light the incense from the candle and place it into the censer(s). Remember that the two pieces of incense should be about four inches apart. If you are using incense on charcoal, add several pinches of incense directly on top of the charcoal. Offer an invocation:

I offer this incense to the Goddess in the Smoke
that she might reveal to me the things
I need to know about what is to be.

If you are using clouds for your divination, it would be more appropriate to say something a little different. If you are performing the divination during the day:

Great God in the Sky, as your light reflects from
the clouds I see, I ask that you reveal to me the
things that I need to know about what is to be.

Under ideal conditions this divination can be performed outside at night as well; it would require a night with a full or nearly full moon and partly cloudy skies. The moon can shine intensely on clouds and illuminate them in ways they don't in daylight. In that case, change the invocation:

Great Goddess, I come to you in your guise as the moon,
daughter of the earth and sister to humankind.

As your light reflects from the clouds I see, I ask that you
reveal to me the things that I need to know about the future.

If indoors, wait a few moments as the smoke begins to develop. From this point, the indoor and outdoor versions of the divination work essentially the same way. If there are specific questions you would like answered, you need to ask them aloud. It is usually less confusing to ask a question and then watch the smoke or clouds for a sign in response before asking the next question. That being said, it is possible to ask a series of questions and then watch for signs for them all. That can be a more conservative use of your time but can make things a bit less clear, especially if some of your questions are completely unrelated.

Even if you don't have specific questions, the divination is still likely to reveal some things to you. This is where our innate ability to interpret shapes and forms, especially ephemeral ones (fleeting shapes that form and dissolve quickly) becomes a powerful tool to understand divination symbols. Best of all, it is so simple. Most of us have watched clouds drift overhead and seen many different shapes that we can easily interpret as animals, plants, and even people. Virtually any object can appear in the smoke or the clouds. Clouds tend to keep their form a lot longer than shapes in incense smoke, so you will need to be especially observant when performing this divination indoors. Where you position the candle is also important. You want the candlelight to illuminate the smoke from below because this tends to give the highest contrast to the smoke.

As you watch the smoke or clouds, take note of any shapes you can identify. If you are pausing between asking questions, write down your question first and then any symbols you might see. If you have asked a group of questions at the same time or if you have asked no questions at all, then simply record anything you see. Whenever you see a shape transform into another recognizable shape, underline or highlight the shapes you see. Those transformations can be the most valuable insights.

If you use incense sticks or cones, your divination will end when the first piece of incense goes out. It's best not to change the smoke source during the divination, so don't try to light an additional stick or cone. Once the divination is complete you can always repeat the entire process if you don't think you received enough information or if something requires additional clarification. Allow the incense or charcoal to burn out before extinguishing the candle.

Once the divination session itself is over you should review the notes you took of what you saw. If your notes include the questions asked, with the symbols you saw before asking the next question, it is a bit easier to identify which symbols are related to which question. Regardless of which approach you prefer, interpretation is a very personal part of this divination. Even if you are asking questions on behalf of other people, it is your interpretation that is critical. Look at your notes and the shapes you saw. How do they relate to you? Are they deeply symbolic, as dreams often are, or do they strike you as literal?

For example, if you asked, "Will there be any major changes in my life in the coming months?" and saw the shape of a horse in the smoke or cloud, it could mean many things. Generally, horses symbolize a wild spirit and freedom. They also represent mobility or travel. It is possible that the symbol you have seen means that you are going to travel or even move. If you grew up with horses, seeing one could represent that part of your childhood or another pastime. It's also possible that the horse isn't as symbolic; it could literally mean that you are going to acquire a horse! How can you tell which of these very different interpretations applies to you? It truly comes back to your perceptions and intuition. Look inside of yourself for the answers. Another person could sit with you throughout the divination and listen to the same questions and away with completely different interpretations. And consider that even if two people sat very close together, they would see the smoke or clouds from different angles; everyone's perspective is different. Always listen to your own instincts when it comes to interpreting the things that are revealed to you through the smoke or clouds. Keep your notes and review them at next year's Imbolc to see how accurate your divination truly was.

RECIPES
AND
CRAFTS

in sheep, cleansing, sprouting seeds, fertility, transitions, protec

rebirth, transformation, youth, well-being, emergence, awakening

nd midpoint between the winter solstice and the vernal equinox,

15 degrees of aquarius in northern hemisphere, sun at 15 degree

thern hemisphere, female; the goddess transforming from crone t

goddess in the form of young mother tending to her growing ch

in the form of a child exploring the world, the innocence of the

Brigid, Aphrodite, Diana, Arianrhod, Artio, Athena, Pa

Inanna, Juno, Selene, Vesta, Delu, Februus, Bragi, Cupid,

Cecht, Dumuzi, Eros, light green: abundance, growth, fertility

lming, new beginnings and prosperity, pink: harmony, tendernes

love, spiritual healing, virtue, spring, honor, contentment, white

eace, protection, healing, truth, divination, purification, childhoo

itality, creativity, communication, the sun, planning, psychic a

angelica: balance, new beginnings, consecration, insight, purificat

uccess, basil: clarity, divination, love, money, protection, streng

erry: growth, attachments, fertility, intuition, prosperity, prote

mon: balance, blessings, courage, protection, purification, strength

$\mathcal{A}$s with any holiday, sabbats usually include food, friendship, and opportunities for crafting items appropriate to the season. Imbolc is no exception. Crafting allows everyone to contribute and participate in the festivities. When food and other items are crafted by participants in the celebration, it infuses the environment with the energies of those participants. It also creates a connection between the festivities and those who help with the crafting.

Imbolc Recipes

The next three recipes can be used together to make a wonderful Imbolc-themed snack table. Some covens and other groups enjoy cakes and ale, although many different foods and drinks are often substituted. When combined with copious amounts of milk, this Imbolc feast can definitely be used in place of cakes and ale. Each recipe can be made independently, and they work perfectly together. You can complete all of the crafting for this feast in less than twenty-four hours. One person can easily do the crafting, but there are some steps that can be done as a group. For the best-tasting results, seek out dairy products that are organic and preferably locally produced. The fresher and more natural the ingredients, the tastier the results.

Yogurt "Cheese"

Imbolc is a sabbat closely associated with milk and milk products. Even simple cheeses are cherished when the first milk of the year is available. You might think of cheese making as a process using strange cultures and esoteric aging techniques. Make no mistake: cheese makers work wonderful magic to produce the astounding variety of cheeses available to us in the twenty-first century. Rather than venture into the mystic realm of cheese making, you can make a very simple cheese with just a few ingredients you might already have on hand. This technique works overnight and requires very little labor. The result is a soft cheesy yogurt similar to cream cheese that can be flavored easily with a variety of savory and sweet ingredients.

Ingredients:

1 quart of unflavored yogurt
   (whole milk yogurt is recommended)
Cheesecloth
A colander or mesh strainer
A small saucer

A bowl large enough to comfortably
  hold the colander or strainer.

Begin by placing the saucer (a jar lid can work as a substitute) upside down in the bottom of the large bowl. Place the colander on top of the inverted saucer. The saucer lifts the colander well above the bottom of the bowl to allow for complete draining. Line the colander with 3–4 layers of cheese cloth. Spoon the yogurt into the colander and place the bowl into the refrigerator overnight.

The next morning you will find that the liquid whey has separated from the yogurt and run into the bottom of the bowl, leaving behind a firm "cheese." Place the bowl on the counter and carefully gather the cheesecloth at the top, enclosing the ball of cheese. Twist the top of the cheesecloth to ensure nothing can squirt out of the top and gently squeeze the cheesecloth from top to bottom to extract any remaining liquid. Expect to extract about half of the yogurt as cheese and half as whey. You can then open the cloth and transfer the cheese to a mixing bowl. The cheesecloth can be washed and reused many times.

The unflavored cheese can be served as it is, but a pinch or two of salt will greatly enhance its flavor. What's even more fun is to make an Imbolc-flavored cheese. For a savory cheese, try adding two tablespoons of dried sweet basil and a teaspoon of salt to the cheese immediately after it is strained. For a fruity option, thaw half a cup (or more) of blackberries and use those in place of the sweet basil. For an even sweeter variant, use half a cup of blackberry preserves or locally harvested honey.

Mix the ingredients thoroughly with a fork. Cover the bowl and return it to the refrigerator until shortly before serving it. For a nicer presentation, once the cheese is chilled again you can gather it back into a ball and then slice the ball in half. Place each half flat-side-down on the center of a serving platter.

Butter

Making butter is easy and something every butter lover should do at least once. You can make butter using a blender, hand blender, hand mixer, or about any other tool that will help you to agitate liquid. You can even make butter using a tightly closed jar!

Ingredients:

a blender or one of the other tools discussed above
a pint or more of heavy cream
a fork
ice cold water
a teaspoon of salt (optional)

Begin by pouring the cream into the blender and "churning" it on a high setting. After several minutes of mixing you will see the cream begin to separate into solid butter and liquid "buttermilk." When you can clearly see the small pieces of butter spinning in the blender you can turn it off. Keep in mind that there is often a thick ring of butter around the blades in the bottom of the blender.

Strain the contents of the blender through a fine sieve or cheese cloth. After straining, place the butter into a bowl and press it with a spoon or spatula until all of the liquid has been extracted. Save the liquid buttermilk for use in the next recipe, for soda bread.

Gather the solid butter together and shape it into a ball or other convenient shape. If you plan to use the butter within a day, you can shape it and return it to the refrigerator to chill. If you want butter that will last much longer, you need to "wash" it. Add at least half (and up to a full) cup of ice-cold water into the bowl with the butter and mix them together. Pour off the water and again press all of the liquid out of the butter. Mix in a teaspoon of salt with a fork, if desired. You can form the butter into many shapes, but a simple approach is to form it into a log shape and wrap it with parchment paper. If you roll the wrapped log back and forth on a smooth surface, you can even out many of its rough edges. Store the butter wrapped in the parchment and it will last a month in a refrigerator (or up to a year in the freezer, if the wrapped butter is placed in a tightly closed plastic bag).

You can add herbs or other flavoring to butter just as you did with the yogurt cheese. Different flavorings can be added to the cold butter and mixed thoroughly with a fork. You can also gently heat the butter and add flavorings to the melted butter to better disperse the flavors.

Soda Bread

This simple and traditional Irish bread requires no yeast and is a tasty way to enjoy the yogurt cheese and butter from the previous two recipes. It is also a great way to use the buttermilk leftover from churning the butter (although you can also use buttermilk purchased from the grocery store).

Ingredients:

3 cups all-purpose flour

1 teaspoon baking soda (use a recently opened
   container, stale soda won't work as well)

1 teaspoon sugar (optional)

2 teaspoon salt (optional)

1 cup buttermilk

Thoroughly mix the powdered ingredients and stir in the buttermilk. Mix with a spoon for one to two minutes and then knead with your hands for another thirty seconds. If the mixture is too dry, moisten it with a little more buttermilk but don't handle the dough any more than is absolutely needed. This dough should be a bit lumpy and wispy, so don't try to make it smooth.

Form the dough into a round shape about eight inches wide. Place it on a cookie sheet that has been covered with parchment paper, or more traditionally, dusted with flour. Press the top flat and then cut the top with a sharp knife. Traditionally you would make two intersecting cuts of equal length across the dough and going about an inch into the sides of the dough in a cross shape. It looks more festive if you make three cuts that create more of a star or asterisk pattern.

Bake the dough at 400° F for 40 to 45 minutes. The top should be brown and the loaf should make a hollow sound when thumped. Remove it from the oven and allow it to cool for fifteen minutes covered with a towel. It can then be served hot or allowed to completely cool before cutting. This traditional bread is filled with tiny pockets and crevices that butter and cheese can fill, making it the perfect centerpiece for your Imbolc feast.

Drinks

Complete the feast with mugs of warm milk or hot cocoa. Alternately, if you and your guests don't find it too chilling, you can make milkshakes by blending ice cream and fresh milk. If you are a little more daring and you enjoy the taste of yogurt, you can make a whey shake by using the whey from the yogurt cheese in place of milk in your shake. Add some vanilla, honey, or blackberries for a tasty and sweet way to finish your feast.

Fortune Cookies

Chinese New Year usually falls within the Imbolc time frame, but even in years where it doesn't, this is a very fun project for any Imbolc celebration. To be fair, the fortune cookie is an American creation and certainly isn't traditional anywhere in Asia. While it might be a bit of a stretch to connect these tasty divination treats with traditional New Year's celebrations, they are still a perfect fit for any Imbolc or New Year's celebration.

You can make fortune cookies for you family and friends or those in your grove or coven. Fortune cookies can be used in divination rituals and can even be used to replace the moon cakes that are traditionally used in many circles. Since you are able to create any fortune you wish, you can even make cookies for specific people (for example, a new parent, a new initiate, a birthday, etc.). There are some fun ideas at the end of this section for how you can involve others in the cookie making, but first let's take a look at the recipe and the simple method for making these awesome cookies.

Ingredients:

4 egg whites

¾ cup sugar

¼ teaspoon salt

9 Tablespoons butter, room temperature

10 Tablespoons all-purpose flour

½ cup ground almond meal

¼ teaspoon vanilla extract

Fortunes or messages on small slips of parchment paper

Wax paper (to protect the fortunes)

Preheat the oven to 350°F. Mix the egg whites and sugar. Once the mixture is well-combined, add the other ingredients one at a time. Mix thoroughly after each ingredient is added. Use a wire whisk to mix the butter thoroughly with the other ingredients. For best results, use a cookie sheet covered with parchment paper. Write the fortunes or messages onto slips of parchment paper and fold several times. These cookies are a bit greasy, so if the fortunes aren't well-wrapped in wax paper the messages might become unreadable.

Once all of the ingredients are completely mixed, measure 1 teaspoon of dough for each cookie and place them 3 to 4 inches apart on the prepared cookie sheet.

Bake for six minutes and remove from the oven. The cookies should be not yet browned on the edges but still one uniform light color. As they bake, they should flatten into a roughly circular shape. If any of your cookies come out uneven, you can use a biscuit cutter make perfect circles. Just be aware that at this stage the cookies are sticky and not very firm, so handle with care.

As soon as you remove the cookies from the oven, place one of the prepared fortunes in the center of each cookie. It's best to put it slightly off-center so the fortune isn't too close to the edge when you fold the cookie. Quickly fold over each cookie to form a half circle that looks a bit like a Chinese dumpling. Use the edge of a butter knife to crimp the edges of the cookie to seal the fortune inside. Parchment paper makes this process easier, since you can lift the paper and put your hand under the cookie when doubling it over. If the center breaks open during the process, crimp that edge as well.

Bake the folded-over cookies for another 6 to 8 minutes. For a consistent color you can flip the cookies over at the 5-minute mark. Finished cookies will be several shades darker than when you removed them to add the fortunes. Remove the cookies from the tray and allow to cool. These cookies are very tasty, so remind people not to eat their fortunes! As you bake each tray of cookies you should keep the uncooked dough in the refrigerator until you are ready to bake.

Making fortune cookies can be a great choice for an Imbolc potluck dinner. They are a great project for an entire group as well. The whole group can join in the process of making one large batch of cookies, with different people doing different parts of the process. Making the cookies as a group means you can bake and fold your cookies and take them directly into a ritual. A fun variation on this is to have everyone bring several fortunes ready to go into the cookies. That way the fortunes are a surprise for everyone. You can even do that if only one or two people bake all of the cookies. Just collect everyone's fortunes and deliver them to the cooks before the baking begins. Remind everyone to carefully wrap their fortunes in wax paper to ensure the messages remain visible once baked in the cookies.

RECIPES AND CRAFTS

Fortune Cookies

Imbolc fortune cookies also make great little gifts. Make a few dozen for friends or co-workers. If you want to add a bit of educational flair, you could put a fortune on one side of the paper and then a Neopagan term and its definition on the reverse side. It's a great way to share some fun (and tasty) cookies with non-Wiccan or non-Pagan friends and share a little knowledge along with the entertainment. It can also be a non-threatening way to introduce a few new ideas to those who may not be knowledgeable about Neopaganism.

You can use this craft for a lot of different magickal or ritual purposes, and it can also be a fun way to break the ice in groups with new members. For instance, if you are teaching a class about tarot, you could put a different major arcana tarot card in each fortune cookie. Pass out the cookies to your students and have them open their cookies one by one and reveal the card within. You can then discuss the card and its various interpretations before having the next person open their cookie and start a discussion about their card.

If you'd like, you can make fortunes very specific. You can even create custom cookie for each person attending your gathering, ritual, or party. If you choose to make cookies for specific people, you'll want to be certain you can identify which cookie should go to which person. The easiest way to do this is for the fortune to have the name of the person (or a number or symbol representing that person) printed on it on at the very end of the slip of paper. When the fortune is placed inside the cookie, leave the name or symbol hanging outside the cookie so you can quickly determine who should receive it.

For most fortune cookies made for Imbolc, you would want fortunes that reflect this celebration. Remember that this is a sabbat focused on new beginnings, birth, and the promise of the coming spring. It is also about being thankful for surviving the cold winter. You can print out your fortunes with a printer and cut them into slips tiny enough to fit inside the cookies. You can also cut small slips of paper and have people handwrite the fortunes. The fortunes might even be as simple as what you personally wish for the person receiving the cookie.

Crafts

Brigid's Cross

Brigid's Cross is a symbol of protection that is traditionally prepared just before Imbolc. Completed crosses are left outside the front door the night before Imbolc in hopes that Brigid will bless them. On Imbolc, the blessed crosses are hung to protect the home. They are often placed near outside doors to prevent misfortune from coming inside. It's a good idea to leave a grain cake or a bit of grass for Brigid's white cow companion—even an oatmeal cookie works great!

Although a Brigid's Cross would traditionally be made from straw taken from the last harvest or from wild-harvested reeds, a variety of modern craft materials can also be used. You can make lovely crosses from materials found at most craft stores, such as pipe cleaners, drinking straws, or strips of colorful paper. Some craft stores also sell straw. You can also find materials in your own yard or the nearest park—straw is just dried grass. You may find some appropriate grass in your yard or flower beds at this time of year that has gone to seed and is dried. This is especially true if you grow any decorative grasses. As long as you have stems at least five inches in length, you can use grass or even dried lavender stems to make your cross.

You will need:

- 9 pieces of straw (or other material as discussed above) of equal length, 3 to 15 inches long

- Thread, string, wire, or rubber bands to tie off the arms of the cross

- A dish or tray large enough to hold your straw while soaking in water (dried materials only)

If you are using straw or other dried materials, begin by soaking them in water for twenty-four hours. If you are using pipe cleaners or other crafting materials, you can skip this step.

If there is still snow on the ground where you live, melt some of it for soaking. The melted snow represents the spring thaw that is soon to come.

After soaking for twenty-four hours, the pieces should be pliable. You should be able to easily bend the straw or stems in half.

1. Cut all of your straw to equal length.

2. Begin with one piece of straw held vertically in one hand.

3. At the center of the first piece, place a horizontal piece of straw, forming a cross.

4. Bend the horizontal piece in the middle to the right so it is doubled over.

5. Rotate the pieces a quarter turn counterclockwise so the doubled-over piece of straw is pointing upwards and the first piece is horizontal.

6. Place a third piece of straw horizontally above the first piece and double it over to the right, so it wraps over the second piece.

7. Rotate the pieces another quarter turn counterclockwise.

8. Double a piece of straw over the center straw towards the right (this will give you cross shape with 4 equal length arms).

9. Continue to rotate the cross counter-clockwise, adding another piece of straw wrapped around the top arm of the cross until all 9 pieces of straw have been used.

10. You should now have a cross with 4 equal arms but if the arms are not of equal length you should cut them now to ensure all arms are the same.

11. Tie off the center of each arm with thread or string (wire or rubber bands may also be used).

Your cross is now ready to be blessed and hung in your home. Keep the crosses up until you replace them with new ones next year.

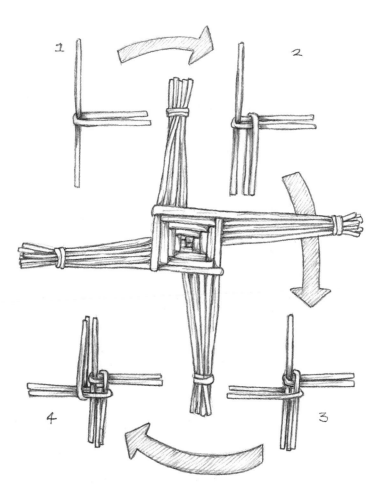

1

2

3

4

Brigid's Cross

Imbolc Incense

Incense making is only as complex as you choose to make it. This is a simple blend of incense that will be heated over charcoal (or in an incense heater or aroma lamp). It works best if the ingredients are powdered, but finely chopped will also work. For ideal results you should make this incense several weeks before Imbolc, but it can still be made on Imbolc if aging it isn't possible.

You will need:

- Cedarwood powder; cedar chips can be substituted if no powder is available, but they must be completely dry—check at pet shops or feed stores if your local metaphysical shop is out of stock

- Dried basil powder is best but not mandatory

- Honey; use local honey if possible and take care to avoid things labeled "honey sauce" or "honey flavored," as those are mostly corn syrup

- A ceramic or paper bowl

- Craft stick; a stout coffee stirrer will also work

- Plastic bag with zipper-style closure

- Small glass or plastic container with tight fitting lid

- Disposable gloves (optional)

Begin by chopping or grinding cedar chips or basil leaves as finely as possible. A coffee grinder or blender can be used, but even a mortar and pestle can be used to grind.

Mix 5 teaspoons chopped or powdered cedar wood with 1 teaspoon dried basil leaves in the bowl.

Stir with the craft stick until the basil is equally distributed in the mixture.

Add a few drops of honey to the mixture. Use *just enough* honey to stick everything together—don't add any more than you have to.

Mix with the craft stick until the honey is evenly distributed. Complete the mixing with your hands if needed, wearing the disposable gloves (latex or otherwise); otherwise wash your hands immediately after you finish mixing.

Once you can gather the incense together in a single ball or glob, drop it into the plastic bag. Close the bag and seal it inside the glass or plastic container. Allow the incense to age until Imbolc.

On Imbolc you should open the sealed container and plastic bag. Pinch off pea-sized balls of incense. If the mixture is still sticky (it takes a week or two for the stickiness to go away), roll the balls in powdered cedar wood or basil to make them easier to handle.

As for use, any time during your preparations for Imbolc or during rituals is great. Remember that it won't burn on its own like a cone or stick of incense. Instead, you will need to heat the incense over charcoal unless you have an incense heater or aroma lamp. If you use an aroma lamp, empty any water and dry the bowl. Then line the bottom of the bowl with a small piece of foil. Light the candle as you normally would and place one of the balls of incense on the foil. The heat from the candle will gently warm the incense so it releases its scent with little or no smoke. The incense can be safely stored in a sealed container for decades.

Dipped Candle Making

There are a variety of ways to make candles: you can hand roll beeswax candles or make floating wick candles or try many approaches in between, but this is a simple and traditional technique. You can use most types of wax you might find in your local craft store, but this approach will also work using paraffin wax from the grocery store. Paraffin wax tends to smoke more than most types of candle wax, but it will still work and can be easily colored.

For the best results, check your local craft or hobby store for soy wax, which melts easily in the microwave so it is the simplest to work with. Just put it into a microwave safe glass container. A container about six inches tall is best. If you use paraffin wax, it is most safely prepared in a double boiler. Remember that wax is flammable and should not come too close to ignition sources. You can purchase wicking specifically for candle making (in a pinch you can use cotton string) along with dyes for candles at many craft or hobby stores. For safest results, especially for novice candle makers, purchase the heaviest wick available. A wick with a wire core will make it easier to straighten candles when they are thin.

Although the end result isn't quite as pure, you can also color candles using wax crayons. Color is an important part of candle magick, so decide the purpose for your candles before you decide on a color. Scenting candle wax requires more instruction than space will allow in this book, but scented wax squares are available at craft store that make it simple. We'll look at one way to scent candles after they are made in the next part of this chapter, on dressing candles.

It is generally easiest and most useful to make white candles, at least for your first batch. Candles made on Imbolc carry special energy, and some people will spend most of this holiday making dozens of candles of different colors. You can use this technique to make candles for use in any of the spells or rituals in this book series.

For this project you will need:

- 1–2 pounds of wax (soy or parrafin)

- 12 or more feet of wicking

- any color or scent squares (optional)

- a rod to hang candles as they cool (a curtain rod, clothes drying rack, or even a sturdy coat hanger works)

This style of dipped candle produces two candles for every wick. You will dip both ends of the wick into the wax at the same time, creating a candle at each end. This technique will produce two candles about five inches long for each cut wick.

Begin by cutting your wick into twelve-inch sections. Most wicks will get a bit longer once soaked with wax so don't be surprised if they stretch. With the wicks cut, heat the wax and color or scent it if you desire. At this point, I would ask for Brigid's blessings as Goddess of the Flame.

I call upon you Brigid, Goddess of the Flame and of the Sacred Well, to bless the candles that I craft today.

I ask that you imbue within them the strength, power, and protection that has helped so many over the millennia.

Come to me Goddess and bless these candles that they will bring your energy and power when called upon.

Thank you, great Goddess.

You might prefer to call to your own deities or even a deity closely identified with your reason for making the candle. For example, if you were making prosperity candles, it would be appropriate to call to Laksmi (goddess of fortune and prosperity) and ask for her energy and blessing.

Candle making is a fun group project as well. You will be amazed at how many candles you can produce in a single afternoon with the help of a few friends—and lots of wax and wick. Chanting and happy conversation will keep positive energy flowing throughout the process.

Remember to prepare your cooling rack so you can hang your candles as you dip them. Begin by holding one of the cut wicks in the center. Allow the ends to hang straight down. Dip the wicks into the melted wax. The wicking may try to float at first, but by dragging the wick back and forth a few times the wax will penetrate the wick and it will sink below the surface. Take care not to put your fingers in the wax. Remove the wick from the wax. The first few times you dip a wick it may wrinkle when it comes of the wax. Gently tug on the ends of the wicking to straighten both ends should this happen. After the wick has been dipped and straightened, hang the wicking over your cooling rack. One candle should hang down on each side. As the candles get larger you should take care that none of the hot candles touch, as they could melt together.

Continue this process until you have used all of your cut wicks. By the time you have finished dipping your last wick, the first set of candles may be cool enough to dip again. Remove the first cooled wick and dip it back into the melted wax. Every time you dip the candles the melted wax adds another layer to the outside of the candle. The first few times you dip the wicks, they may not seem like they are changing, but continue the process and they will begin to get larger before your eyes. For candles five inches long, you should dip them until they are a half to three-quarters of an inch in diameter.

You may have to reheat your soy wax periodically. Just place the container in the microwave for a minute and make certain you remove any stray wicking from the container before microwaving. Paraffin candles can be dipped directly from the double boiler so the wax is always hot.

Once the candles have cooled, you can cut and trim the wicks to size or leave the candles in pairs until they are needed. You can also carve, decorate, and dress the candles any way you would like. You will find that candles you make on Imbolc will be amazing sources of energy throughout the year.

Candle Dressing

The simplest way to make a dramatic change to a candle is "dressing," a technique that adds both the scent and plant energy. Dressing uses essential oils, often undiluted. As many undiluted oils can be very harsh on skin, many people wear disposable gloves whenever handling these oils in their concentrated form. Essential oils that have been added to a carrier oil (a benign oil such as sweet almond or olive that dilutes essential oils) are generally safe for bare skin but you should still keep contact to a minimum.

To dress a candle, the sides (and occasionally the top) of the candle are lightly coated in essential oil. As the candle warms from the flame, it heats the oils on the candle. The oils usually dissipate long before the flame reaches them, so candles can be dressed more than once. The easiest way to dress a candle without touching the oil is to use a cotton swab, paper towel, or soft cloth. Drizzle a small amount of oil onto the side of the candle or onto the cloth or towel. Use the swab, towel, or cloth to spread the oil evenly across the surface of the candle. Any cloth or paper towel used to spread the oil will retain its scent for a long time. You might use it as a room freshener until the last trace of scent is gone. You might wish to blend several different essential oils for dressing your candle. Try to mix the oils several days in advance and put the mix into a sealed container. Shake or stir the contents once or twice a day to ensure that the oils blend completely.

You can also find special paints in many hobby or craft stores that allow you to paint decorations on your candles. You can also use a sharp blade to carve symbols or words into a candle. You can accomplish much the same thing with a heated nail carefully held in a pair of pliers. There are lots of creative ways to make a purchased candle unique to you and your goals.

Corn Dollies

There are about as many ways to make corn dollies as there are to make chili! Corn dollies are often associated with harvest festivals but they are traditionally made at Imbolc as well. At Imbolc they may be made from straw from the last harvest of the previous year or from reeds or grasses collected just before Imbolc. While you may not have a marsh in your backyard where you can collect reeds, many of us can find suitable plant materials outdoors (assuming they aren't buried under snow). Many of the grasses grown for decorative purposes are wonderful for making this style of corn dolly. Look for grass (usually brown and dry at Imbolc) with seed heads on them. They should be about as sturdy as the bristles on a new broom when bunched together. If you cut some down and look at the cut ends you should see that they have a hole or appear hollow at the end. Those stems may be the perfect solution. Look for stems without seed heads too. As long as they are equally sturdy, you can use them along with the seed heads.

For a more urban solution, visit your local craft store. Those stores often sell dried plants and flowers for decorative purposes. Look for the same characteristics you would in the wild; remember that anything you buy in a craft store should be properly dried, clean, and ready before using. Straw and other dried materials can be used but you should try to find at least one dried stalk with a large seed head for every corn dolly you want to make. Get a dozen stalks or more for each corn dolly. Straw is usually compressed so the straw itself is flat rather than round. You can work with this straw but you still need at least on stalk with a seed head, even if that stalk looks different from the rest of the straw that you use.

Gather between ten and fifteen stalks, and cut them to equal length. Most of the stalks will be bent in half to form the body and legs of the dolly. The remaining stalks will form the dolly's arms. Using a shallow pan (such as a cookie sheet) large enough to hold the stalks, soak them in warm water overnight except for any stalks with seed heads, which will be used for the head and don't need to be flexible. After soaking, the stalks should be flexible where you can easily bend and twist them without breaking. If not, continue soaking until they can be easily bent. Flattened straw from a straw bale may already be flexible enough to use without soaking.

Leaving 3 to 4 stalks behind, gather a handful of the stalks into a bundle and grasp the bundle in the middle with one hand. Double the bundle over at the midpoint to form the body of the corn dolly. Hold the bottom half of the doubled-over bundle to keep the stalks in place. With your other hand insert the stalk with the seed head down through the center of the doubled-over bundle. The base of the seed head should be slightly above the top of the doubled-over bundle. The ends of the stalks should be at the bottom and the seed head at the top to represent the dolly's head.

While holding the doubled-over bundle with the seed head in one hand, use the other hand to pick up the remaining 3 to 4 softened strands. Use those remaining strands to form the dolly's arms by tying them horizontally around the upper body of the corn dolly, about a third of the way down from the base of the seed head. Wrap the strands all the way around the bundle at least once and leave the ends protruding out like outstretched arms. If your strands will keep the shape, you can even pose the arms into different positions. You may need to tie the arms into a knot to keep them in place if the strands aren't stiff enough. You can also use a little thread or twine to tie the bundle together and hold the arms in place. This is a traditional female corn dolly.

To make it a male dolly, separate the bottom part of the bundle into two distinct pieces to represent legs. You may need to tie the legs at the bottom to keep them apart. Remember that at Imbolc, female corn dollies are made to represent Brigid and her blessings of warmth and light. Making male corn dollies isn't a traditional Imbolc activity.

With such an abundance of crafting materials, you can create quite an impressive Imbolc altar. The bread, cheese, and other edibles will make a wonderful centerpiece to an altar covered with a white or yellow cloth. Adding an arrangement of fresh flowers from the season, such as daffodils or crocuses, will help to bring life energy to it. Including an assortment of candles and at least one corn dolly and one Brigid cross to your altar will result in a stunning Imbolc altar, filled with offerings for this wonderful sabbat.

Corn Dollies

119
......
RECIPES AND CRAFTS

PRAYERS
AND
INVOCATIONS

...m sleep, cleansing, spreading roots, fertility, transitions, prote...
... rebirth, transformation, youth, well-being, emergence, awakening...
...ual midpoint between the winter solstice and the vernal equinox...
...15 degrees of aquarius in northern hemisphere, sun at 15 degre...
...thern hemisphere, female; the goddess transforming from crone t...
...goddess in the form of young mother tending to her growing ch...
...en the form of a child exploring the world, the innocence of th...
...Brigid, Aphrodite, Diana, Arianrhod, Artio, Athena, Da...
...Inanna, Juno, Selene, Vesta, Belu, Februus, Bragi, Cupid...
...Ecohl, Dumuzi, Eros, light green: abundance, growth, fertility...
...ining, new beginnings and prosperity, pink: harmony, tendernes...
... love, spiritual healing, virtue, spring, honor, contentment, white...
...eace, protection, healing, truth, divination, purification, childhoo...
...utility, creativity, communication, the sun, planning, psychic a...
...angelica: balance, new beginnings, consecration, insight, purificat...
...success, basil: clarity, divination, love, money, protection, streng...
...erry: growth, attachments, fertility, intuition, prosperity, prote...
...mon: balance, blessings, courage, protection, purification, strength...

$\mathcal{W}$ORKING WITH DEITIES or natural energies doesn't always require complex rituals or complex spells. Oftentimes a simpler approach will provide you with those contacts in just a few moments, usually without the need for any tools other than yourself. The following invocations, prayers, meditations, and simple magicks can provide you with clarification, direction, and a deeper connection with both the natural and supernatural worlds.

Blessings for New Projects

As Imbolc is a time for planning new projects, it is also a great time to ask for blessings for your new (and renewed) projects. The following prayer to the elephant-headed Hindu god Ganesha can help remove obstacles blocking the success of your projects in the coming warmer days. Ganesha is known as Lord of New Beginnings, which makes this a perfect prayer for Imbolc.

Ganesha is a very approachable god and a powerful ally for any new project. That being said, Ganesha is also a god who will become offended if we ask for his help *after* having asked others before him. Ganesha wants to be the first god on your list, so offer this prayer before invoking other deities and—if you use one—before casting a magick circle. Just be certain that Ganesha is the deity in your workings since he is also known as Lord of Obstacles (he can remove them but he can also place them in your way)! If you wish to make an offering, Ganesha is very fond of cakes made of grain (a rice cake or corn muffin would make a good substitute). If you choose to use offer a candle, use one that is pink or white.

> Great Lord Ganesha, I call upon you at this
> season of Imbolc and ask for your blessings
> and thank you for hearing my plea.
>
> Lord Ganesha, I ask your blessings on
> [my new project] in the coming year.
>
> Please grant your favor and remove all obstacles
> that stand in the way of my / our success.
>
> I ask that you show me / us the path to success.
>
> I thank you for listening to my prayer.

If you have used a candle or incense as your offering, it is best to allow it to burn completely. If you are doing other rituals, prayers, or meditations, allow the candle or incense to burn

PRAYERS AND INVOCATIONS

as a continuing blessing for all the other work you do. Safety is an important concern here, and you should never leave anything unattended while it burns. If you can't stay nearby until the offering has burned out, allow it to burn as long as you safely can. Food offerings can be left outside to feed some of the Earth's hungry animals who are also just beginning to emerge from winter's icy grip.

Prayers for Healing

Brigid is a goddess of healing, and Imbolc is a time for new beginnings, so this sabbat is a perfect occasion to call upon her powers to heal body and mind. Whether physical or emotional healing is needed, her energies have long been revered for healing of all kinds. A white candle is often used when praying to Brigid, but a blue candle is also appropriate when asking for healing. Be aware that many Pagans and Wiccans believe that when praying for another, the other person's permission should always be granted beforehand. Praying for the wellbeing of others seems like a kindness, but it is wise to ask before sending any type of energy to another person.

A Prayer for Healing the Body

Physical injury and illness are simply part of life, but winter adds its own season of physical issues. Endless days spent indoors while waiting for warmer days makes illness spread more easily.

For many of us, the cold aggravates old injuries, and the ice and snow in many places also increases the number of injuries. Imbolc is a great time to energize healing of these physical ailments. Light a candle and ask Brigid to help. You can always ask for general health, but the energy will be more focused if your healing request is specific.

> Goddess Brigid, Maiden, Mother, and Crone,
> protector of life, I ask that you return health to me /
> [name other people] during this season of Imbolc.
>
> Please send your healing power to mend bone
> and flesh, ease breathing, and restore full life.
>
> Above all else, please ease the pain and
> discomfort until health is restored.
>
> Glorious Brigid, goddess of flame and of well,
> in the light of perfect love, bring a swift
> healing to those who are suffering.

A Prayer for Healing the Mind, Heart, or Soul

Those close quarters of the cold days can also cause rifts between us and those closest to us. Sometimes new beginnings are created because something else has come to an end. Getting a new job is a type of a new beginning, but sometimes the new job came about after losing a previous job, or it means leaving behind coworkers with whom you had grown close. Starting a romantic relationship with someone is a new beginning, but often new relationships come about after the ending of previous ones. Just as old physical injuries can leave us with scars and chronic pain, old emotional pain can linger for a lifetime if left unaddressed. Light your candle and ask Brigid to use her immense power to help heal minds as well as bodies.

Goddess Brigid, Keeper of the Flame, Tender of the Well,
I come to you to ask for the healing of an injured soul.

Please look into deepest places within [person's name]
and find the injuries that lie beneath the surface.

I ask that you ease the pain within my / that soul.

Just as this candle shines, I ask that you
shine a light on a path towards healing.

Shine a light so bright and clear that
the path to healing is unmistakable.

Please send whatever assistance will be
needed to make this soul whole once again.

Opening to New Possibilities

Much of the focus of Imbolc is on new life and new beginnings. We understand that the wheel of the year turns and life begins anew, so Imbolc always has these themes. That doesn't mean that you are going to launch new projects or start new relationships every year, however. Sometimes we grow so comfortable in our lives that we stop even considering the possibility of change. The following meditation is one way to open yourself to new possibilities that might not normally be on your radar, so to speak.

The heart of meditation is to quiet your mind. While the kind of contemplative meditation in this exercise will not completely quiet the mind, it can create a serene space where new possibilities can reveal themselves. Sadly, our inner voice is sometimes so quiet that we can't hear its whispers above the voices outside ourselves. Meditation can help to hear those faint voices.

If possible, select a location to meditate where you have a clear view of a natural space, such as an open field, a stand of trees, or even a snow covered patch of yard. You don't have to be physically outside (you could look out a window or even use a photo of an appropriate scene), but if you can comfortably sit for a while outside that can add to the experience. Physical discomfort can distract from your ability to quiet your mind, so sit somewhere comfortable. Don't get too comfortable, or when you relax your mind you might accidentally fall asleep!

Look out on the barren or frozen landscape of late winter. As you begin to still your mind, let your gaze drift around the scene. If you live in an urban area, you might use an empty lot that grows a little patch of weeds each summer. In rural areas you might look out over a brown pasture or a grove of deciduous trees bare of leaves. Even a planter on your porch with a patch of snow where flowers will bloom in the summer is a good focal point.

Just take in your view of the life that is about to emerge from winter's grip. As you allow your own voice to fade away, let that natural space fill your mind. If you have trouble quieting your inner conversation you might try singing a verse of a favorite song or chanting for a minute or two to help silence your thoughts. As you look at your bit of natural landscape, allow your mind to start to see its future. See the snow melting, the brown grass turning green and growing under a summer sun, or see flowers sprouting from the window box outside. As you watch this bit of nature turn the wheel of the year, relax your mind and allow images to enter into the scene.

Many times you might see only the growth that comes with the turning of the wheel, but if you keep your mind open you may well see signs of new possibilities for yourself. It might be something as obvious as the revelation of a new garden spot in your yard. It might be something more esoteric such as seeing yourself in the landscape performing some task. You may even receive a visit from a spirit guide to nudge you in a certain direction. The more subtle signs may require a great deal of thought and reflection to decipher. Often during this type of meditation people will have a "Eureka!" moment of clarity where a new possibility suddenly becomes obvious. Don't worry if you have no such moments. There isn't always a need for new opportunities, and that result might tell you that you are already on a good path.

Prophecies of Faunus

Faunus (also known as Lupercus) is the center of the Lupercalia festival discussed in the Old Ways chapter. He is renowned for bringing prophetic dreams to those who ask him or sleep in his sacred places. You should be warned, however, that Faunus has an untamed energy that can result in frightening or upsetting dreams even when they may portend wonderful things. Unless you are very familiar with interpreting dreams, those sent by Faunus may be difficult to comprehend. Faunus does not communicate verbally; instead, he uses very primal energies and symbols to convey any messages.

If Faunus grants you a dream, write down as many details as possible as soon as you wake. He is a protective deity but his animalistic methods of protection can sometimes be difficult for humans to understand. For instance, he protects livestock from wolves *and* at the same time protects wolves from humans. His sense of balance is nature-based and doesn't always agree with the human perspective. You may have to review the details of the dream many times to gain real insight to its meaning. His symbols may be violent or sexual, making it even more difficult to see a positive interpretation, but the dreams are famed for their powerful truths.

While it is unlikely that you will want to sleep beneath a holly tree, open a window in your bedroom—if only a tiny crack. Doing so will provide an easy pathway to Faunus's natural energies. If you believe the god Pan has appeared in a dream after you have reached out to Faunus, carefully evaluate the dream; Faunus is often mistaken for Pan.

Just before going to bed on the night of the full moon or the new moon, quiet your mind and call to this ancient god.

Faunus, Wild One, Lupercus, god to the fathers
of the Romans, I ask you to hear my words.

Show me what the future holds
for me in the coming long days.

Your strength, your passion, and your
essence of nature can open the eyes
of a human to possibilities that might
never be considered otherwise.

I call upon you to enter my heart
and look upon my soul this night.

Guide my dreams and show me what lies ahead.

If you don't receive a prophetic dream on the first night, don't give up! Offer the invocation the next night at the exact same time of night. If you continue every night for twenty-eight days, you will have performed the invocation in every phase of the moon. If Faunus hasn't sent a dream to you by then, accept that perhaps he has nothing to show you. You can try again at a later date.

Chinese Red Envelopes

It is traditional in China to give red envelopes (called *hong bao* or *lai see*) as gifts for weddings and birthdays, but they are most frequently given during Chinese New Year. The social rules in China for giving envelopes are well-defined and somewhat rigid. Adults give them to children in their lives and those who regularly provide goods or services (much like in America you might give a small gift to your letter carrier or newspaper delivery person). They are not given to peers or those in a more powerful position than the giver. For example, an employer will traditionally give employees a red envelope during New Year's, but an employee would never give an envelope to the employer. Parents traditionally give them to adult children if they are single, but not much beyond their mid-twenties.

Inside the envelopes is a single, dependable item: money. The amount depends upon the relationship you have with the person to whom you give it. The closer the connection to the person receiving the envelope, the more money would be given. While such rules don't translate perfectly into Western terms, it is some-what similar to some traditions where money is given to children at Christmas or on birthdays with lesser amounts given based on the "distance" of the relation (for example, your uncle would give you more money as a Christmas gift than your great uncle). We can take the core idea, adapting it to a new practice that borrows from this long-held Eastern tradition, and blend it into a Western context. While some might appreciate a tradition of handing out money to family and friends around Imbolc every year, there's a different, more personal gift you can give to those who matter to you—some may say it is a better gift than a few dollar bills.

Rather than giving envelopes to "subordinates," these enve-lopes can just as easily be given to anyone important in your life—especially anyone you interact with regularly. Rather than offering cash or gift cards as is so common during some holi-days, you can celebrate the Chinese New Year, or even Imbolc itself, by giving envelopes that contain a simple phrase about what the receiver of the envelope means in your life. There are many times when we become connected to people in our day-to-day lives, and they never have any idea how they affect you. The grocery store clerk who always asks how your children are, the neighbor who tosses your newspaper onto your porch when it's raining, and your child's teachers might all be people who make a regular, positive effect on your life. They will probably have no idea that their small services and kindnesses are mean-ingful unless you tell them. The red envelope is a great way.

The envelopes are red to represent good luck for the coming year, so it's worth the extra effort to shop for red envelopes but not mandatory. Place a small card inside each envelope with a single hand-written sentence telling the addressee how they positively touch your life. "Your smile always brightens my day" or "You can always make me laugh" are the types of messages you can send to others that show you've noticed their efforts—and there's no need to stop there, either.

How often do we stop and tell the people who matter the most to us how much we appreciate the little things they do for us? Sometimes people feel they're being taken for granted when they make the effort to do little things but are never acknowledged. Even if they don't feel that way, giving them a red envelope is a great way to warm the heart of someone close to you just by letting them know you noticed. You can also use these envelopes to reward a child for an accomplishment, even if only a small one.

Each red envelope should be hand-labeled (and addressed if being mailed) with a single card enclosed. A red index card is a good choice, but any color or style is fine. The Chinese dragon is a symbol of good fortune, so a card featuring one would be doubly blessed. You could even use a blank greeting card. Write a single phrase on the card that succinctly tells the person one way she or he makes your life better.

Each card should be written by hand, and no two cards should say exactly the same thing. Give thought to each card and avoid mundane, impersonal phrases like "Thank you for picking up my paper." Dig deeper into what the person does. For example:"Every time I find my newspaper safe and dry on the porch, I know that you are out there in the rain thinking about me, and that makes my day a little brighter." After each envelope is sealed, place both hands over it and invoke an appropriate goddess or god to bless the envelope and its contents. Choose a goddess or god based on what you have written on the card for that particular person. For the example cited earlier, if a person made you feel safer you might ask Kwan Yin (a patron goddess of guardians) to bless the envelope.

You can also make this bit of personal magick quite a surprise if you hand envelopes out on the first day of the Chinese New Year. Outside of large cities with active Asian communities, many of us in the West are unaware of the date, as it changes every year. The envelope will be a complete surprise for most. This type of small recognition and blessing can multiple many times as that energy radiates out to those around the person who received your blessing.

RITUALS
OF
CELEBRATION

...m sleep, cleansing, sprouting seeds, fertility, transitions, protec...

..., rebirth, transformation, youth, well-being, emergence, awakening...

...nial midpoint between the winter solstice and the vernal equinox,...

...15 degrees of aquarius in northern hemisphere, sun at 15 degre...

...thern hemisphere, female; the goddess transforming from crone t...

...goddess in the form of young mother tending to her growing c...

...en the form of a child exploring the world, the innocence of th...

...Brigid, Aphrodite, Diana, Arianrhod, Artio, Athena, Da...

...Inanna, Juno, Selene, Vesta, Febu, Februus, Bragi, Cupid,...

...Cocht, Dumuzi, Eros, light green: abundance, growth fertility...

...aling, new beginnings and prosperity, pink: harmony, tenderness...

...love, spiritual healing, virtue, spring, honor, contentment, white...

...peace, protection, healing, truth, divination, purification, childho...

...vitality creativity, communication, the sun, planning, psychic a...

...angelica: balance, new beginnings, consecration, insight, purificat...

...success, basil: clarity, divination, love, money, protection, streng...

...berry: growth, attachments, fertility, intuition, prosperity, prot...

...amon: balance, blessings, courage, protection, purification, streng...

*I*F YOU WANT to extend your Imbolc magick and celebration beyond simple invocations, you might consider a more elaborate ritual. While full rituals are generally more complicated in preparation and execution, they also provide a deeper, more effective experience. There are three different rituals in this chapter. The first is a Solitary ritual, the second is intended for couples, and the third is for covens or other groups. Although these rituals are carefully designed to be as flexible as possible, feel free to make whatever changes are needed to make them fit with your needs and beliefs.

The Fire Seed: A Solitary Ritual

Imbolc is truly a perfect time to take the flame we light as the earth turns toward spring and internalize it as well as celebrate it. The idea of a "fire seed" is to plant within you a burning energy that will grow and blossom in the spring or summer. My father might have referred to this ritual as "setting a fire under your backside" rather than a fire seed, but the ideas are essentially the same. This ritual is for a solitary practitioner, and with good reason.

Many of us have experience using magick as a tool to ask for things we want. Using magick to attract money is an ancient practice that is likely to continue as long as there is a concept of money, but it is often focused on *want* rather than *need*. A fire seed can be used for a want, but it serves very little purpose; you already have the drive and desire for the things you want. Fire seeds are more about what you need—but likely don't want.

A perfect example of when to use a fire seed would be a habit you wish to break. They can be used for many different purposes, but breaking a habit is one use most of us can relate to. You might know that you should stop smoking cigarettes but in your heart you just don't have the desire. Although you want to stop, there are times when other factors (like addiction) might pull you back to your habit. Maybe you are excited about taking a new college class but it is only available at 7:00 on Monday mornings. A fire seed can help motivate you to roll out of bed in time to make that class. Maybe you want to write the "Great American novel" but you can't seem to find time to do it.

Using a fire seed will help create a "burning desire" within you that you can draw upon when needed. Imbolc is the time to plant seeds of any sort, and it is an ideal time for planting a fire seed within yourself. Fire seeds are often kept a private matter (unlike the traditional New Year's resolution). If your fire seed is growing and helping you, the only change others might observe is a change in your habits.

A word of caution is warranted: you have probably heard the phrase "Be careful what you wish for, you just might get it." That's definitely true with fire seeds. Don't create a fire seed without thinking about all the possible effects. If you plant a fire seed to find time to write your novel, could it have a negative effect on your romantic or family relationships, for example? A fire seed can continue to have influence even when it becomes very inconvenient. You can sometimes extract or extinguish one, but it is much better to think your wish through in advance and never try to plant more than one fire seed at a time.

This ritual is best done within the confines of a magick circle. Even if you do not normally work within a circle, creating one is strongly advised for this ritual because you want to take care that no stray energies are present when you plant your fire seed. As with any magick, this ritual can be performed with no tools except for yourself, but it does benefit from the use of certain altar tools if they are available.

......

- *A piece of paper*—this should have written on it what you want your fire seed to do. Try to make the goal simple; avoid writing more than one sentence. For example, "Make me want to quit smoking" or "Give me courage" to do a specific task. Write clearly so that you can easily read it.

- *Cauldron*—a dark-colored dish or cup made of ceramic, metal, or earthenware can be used.

- *Athame*—a kitchen knife can be used instead, but you should use a dull knife (like a butter knife) and its handle should be wrapped with something black. Alternatively, you can substitute a wand.

- *Chalice*—you can use any clear drinking glass.

- *Liquid*—while a small amount of liquor works well, that isn't appropriate for everyone. Use hot tea or hot water if you prefer.

- *Small White Candle & Holder*—this can be as simple as a small white birthday candle atop a small saucer or a white tea light candle in a glass candleholder. A candle you have made yourself or one you have previously enchanted is best.

- *Altar table*—this needn't be a dedicated altar; it can be any small table you can use while standing.

It should be large enough to hold the items you will use in the ritual but small enough that you can easily walk in a circle all the way around it.

- *White altar cloth*—any clean white cloth will do. It doesn't have to be something used exclusively in rituals.

- *Lighter or matches*—you will light the candle during the ritual.

- If you have difficulty standing or kneeling for more than a few minutes, consider placing a chair or stool near the altar. You might also want tongs or pliers for holding the paper as you ignite it.

Imbolc is a perfect time to plant a fire seed, and at this time of year, Brigid is the obvious deity to ask for help and power in this ritual. You could certainly substitute (or add) deities from your own path, but asking Brigid on Imbolc certainly puts some extra power into the process. If you modify the ritual for another deity, be certain to rewrite the incantations to apply specifically to the deity to call to help you.

Clean and cleanse the space where you will perform the ritual. Physically cleaning your space is both a sign of respect to the deities you will invite into the space and minimizes distractions that might draw your mind away from the ritual. For cleansing, use a good incense or smudge bundle to expel all the unwanted energies from your space. Remember that negative or unwanted energies accumulate in daily life, so clean and cleanse the space any time you plan to work with a fire seed to ensure that no unintended energy is taken inside of you.

Place your cloth on your altar table, followed by the tools you need. The cauldron and chalice should be on the left (west) side of your altar table. Leave your cauldron empty. Your athame and/or wand should go on the right (east) side. Your (as yet unlit) candle should be placed in its holder in the center of the altar. Place the piece of paper with your fire seed desire written on it in front of the candle in its holder. Finally, add your liquid to the chalice. If using hot water or tea, be sure that it is not so hot that you will burn yourself. Do not fill the chalice to the top. You only need an inch or two of liquid, especially if you are using alcohol.

You may use the following Call to Quarters or use your path's method for casting a magick circle. Remember that although we call them "circles," they are actually spheres. This is especially important for rituals like this one where you will stand and raise your arms. You want to be certain that your sphere is large enough to allow you to raise your arms without touching its edges.

Magick circles are usually "called" by asking the four elements to join together. The elements are each associated with a direction on the compass. Some Pagans align their circles with true north (meaning pointing at the actual northern "top" of the planet) while others align their circles with magnetic north (which drifts from time to time). There are four "cardinal" points marking the boundaries of the circle. When going clockwise around the circle (often called "deosil"), the east is the element of Air, south is Fire, west is Water, and north is Earth.

To call the quarters, walk all the way around your altar once, staying near the outside edge but always within the circle. You may want to trace the outer edge of the circle using your athame or wand. If you use one of those tools, put it back on the altar table before moving on to the next step. Begin at the eastern quarter and walk one complete circle. When you return to the eastern quarter, face towards the outside of the circle, still standing within the circle/sphere. Raise your arms and offer the following (or similar) evocation:

> *Spirits of the East, great Powers of Air, I call*
> *you to my circle tonight and ask that you join*
> *me for the important work that I do here.*
>
> *Please bring your wisdom and whimsy to this*
> *circle and inspire my working here tonight.*

Continue to the other quarters and repeat the process with these evocations:

Spirits of the South, great Powers of Fire,
I call you to my circle tonight and ask that you
join me for the important work that I do here.

Please bring your strength and energy to this
circle and guard my workings here tonight.

Spirits of the West, great Powers of Water,
I call you to my circle tonight and ask that you
join me for the important work that I do here.

Please bring your compassion and fearless
embrace of change to this circle and
enlighten my workings here tonight.

Spirits of the North, great Powers of Earth,
I call you to my circle tonight and ask that you
join me for the important work that I do here.

Please bring your power and reason to this circle
and enhance my workings here tonight.

Once you have called the quarters, continue around the altar
clockwise until you are standing in the southern quarter of your
circle. Turn and face your altar and offer this invocation:

Goddess Brigid, Goddess of Fire and Water, I call you
and invite you to the circle I have cast this night.

Goddess of the Sacred Well and Keeper of Flames,
I ask that you bring your power and wisdom to this circle
tonight, to put your flame and energy into the fire seed
that I create tonight to help it thrive and grow.

Brigid, Goddess of the Forge, I honor you and ask for
your help and enlightenment in my work tonight.

Light the candle and say:

I come here tonight to ask for
change in the form of a fire seed.
Goddess Brigid, help me to form and implant
this seed, that great things might grow from it.

Pick up the piece of paper and say:

I create this fire seed tonight with the sole
purpose of [read what you have written.]

Read slowly and clearly to ensure there is no confusion about what the fire seed is going to do. Fold the paper into a triangle shape that is small enough to fit inside your cauldron but large enough that you can safely maintain your grip on the paper while holding it in the candle's flame.

Once the paper is folded, hold it tightly in your dominant hand while you focus your gaze on the candle. Focus your mind on the fire seed's goal. Visualize the fire seed inside of you, performing its task perfectly. See it in your mind's eye as a small red sphere that glows brightly with Brigid's flame inside of it. Continue to meditate and visualize until you feel the energy of the fire seed that you are creating. At the moment when you can easily feel the energy, place one corner of the triangular-folded paper in the candle's flame while saying:

I call to you Brigid, Goddess of Fire and Water,
to set these words into the heart of my fire seed.

This fire seed shall not dim until its
goal has been fully realized.

So mote it be!

Place the burning paper in your cauldron. As the paper is consumed by fire, visualize your new fire seed rising from the ashes with heat and brightly glowing light. When the paper is totally consumed, the fire seed will be fully empowered and ready for tempering.

This next step will harden the outside of the fire seed to give it longevity. It will also reduce the heat from Brigid's flame enough that you can safely take it within you. Tempering the fire seed will require you to move it, but you cannot physically touch the fire seed: it is a symbolic construction that does not fully exist on the physical plane. However, you can move it by placing your hands on either side of the cauldron that contains the newly formed fire seed.

With your thoughts focused only on moving the fire seed, lift your hands above the cauldron to draw the fire seed out. Move your fire seed slowly until you are holding it above your chalice. Then say:

> *The seed has been empowered with Fire, but may it also be*
> *tempered, just as the blacksmith tempers steel, and blessed*
> *with the powers of Water so that the seed will never burn me.*

Release the fire seed to drop into the chalice. Take a deep breath and lift the chalice above eye level and say:

> *Within this blessed chalice the fire seed is ready.*
>
> *I ask that all Powers gathered in this circle*
> *tonight bless and empower this seed to help me to*
> *achieve its goal while causing no harm to others.*
>
> *The seed will now become part of*
> *who I am, as I take its flame inside me.*
>
> *So mote it be.*

As quickly as you can, drink the liquid in the chalice. If possible, drink the liquid (with the fire seed inside of it) in a single effort. When you have finished drinking all of the liquid you can end the ritual:

The seed is within me and I feel its heat even now.

It will stay burning within me
until its goal has been achieved.

Thank you Goddess Brigid for sharing your
flame and your water with me tonight, that
I might make this change within myself.

I emerge from this circle a person reborn, with
this fire seed glowing inside of my very heart.

Return the empty chalice to its place on your altar. If you have other magickal work that you would like to do, you can continue using this circle until you are finished with all of your workings. You may then banish your magick circle using the techniques of your path. If you have used the circle calling that I have included in the ritual, you can banish the circle according to the following:

First release any deities you may have invoked (aside from Brigid) and then release Brigid herself:

Great Brigid, Goddess of the Flame and Goddess of the
Well, I thank you for joining this magick circle tonight and
for the energy and wisdom you have bestowed upon me.

I release you from this circle and ask only that you listen for
my voice and rejoin my circle when next I call your name.

Walk around your altar deosil (clockwise) until you reach the Northern quarter. Facing outward from your altar, release the Northern quarter first:

Spirits of the North, Great powers of Earth,
I open this magick circle and release you.

Stay if you will, go if you must.

Then walk counterclockwise (also called "widdershins") to the western quarter and repeat the process for the element of Water. Continue on to release the southern and eastern quarters as well. Finally say:

The circle is open but never broken.

Magick is afoot tonight.

Dispose of the ash in your cauldron into running water or bury it in your yard. For those who practice incense magick, you can also sift the ash and add it to your primary magickal censer.

New/Renewed Love: A Ritual for Couples

February is a month associated with love and romance as well as fertility. This is a ritual intended to affirm—or reaffirm—the love between two people. The ritual is written in a nongender-specific way so it can be used by any couple. Love is not bound by conventional wisdom or social influence, so it's important that the magick of love is also unbound. Love can also exist as a platonic emotion, so you could even use this ritual (with some slight modification) for any two people, not just lovers.

As with all rituals you read in this series of books, you can and should modify the rituals to fit your spiritual path and personal beliefs. This ritual in particular should be modified to fit you precisely. The spoken portion of this spell should be rewritten specifically for you and the other person in your ritual. The words that follow are suggestions only since this is such a highly personal ritual. This ritual is appropriate for Imbolc itself, but it is also appropriate for any time during the Milk Moon (usually during Imbolc) or even on the secular holiday of Valentine's Day. Choose a time when the two of you can be together without interruptions. That can be a real feat if you have children in the house, but a few minutes to devote only to your lover is a wonderful gift for you both.

For this ritual you will need the following items:

- A red or pink taper (with holder) or pillar candle

- 2 white taper candles and holders

- Essential oils or two small sticks of incense representing each participant (use only a few drops of each scent). Participants should select an oil or incense with which they strongly identify. If you choose incense, you will also need an incense heater. One filled with ash or sand is best.

- A chalice; a nice wine glass makes a good chalice.

- Two small glasses, preferably with a pouring spout, like a measuring cup; you will pour from them.

- Drinking liquids, one liquid representing each person.

- An altar cloth that is pleasing to both participants (white cloth is always appropriate, but a pink or red cloth would work as well)

- Gentle music in the background; optional, but can enhance the atmosphere

- Both participants should also bring a small item that reminds them of the other person.

- Coffee stirrer, wooden craft stick, or mixing spoon (optional)

- Small cloth for dressing candles; use if your chosen essential oils are not suspended in a carrier or base oil (optional)

Performing this ritual in the light of the moon adds even more energy and excitement. You don't have to wait for a full moon, however; the light of a crescent moon is still potent, and, of course the moon itself is a powerful symbol to many lovers. I recommend doing this particular ritual skyclad (no clothing), but don't do anything in any ritual that makes you significantly uncomfortable. Going skyclad isn't for everyone, but if you've never tried it before, this would be a good first skyclad ritual.

If you and your lover have never done magick together before, it's a really good idea to have a discussion about how you want to proceed. This ritual can be done within a magick circle, but it is not a requirement. You may wish to invite your personal deities into the ritual or perform it just as written. As long as both of you are in agreement, you can make as many modifications to this ritual as you both would like.

Begin by dimming the lights and turning off your phones. If music is available, turn it on before starting. While this ritual is intended to be a gentle time between lovers (thus gentle music is recommended), if heavy metal is more the style for you and your lover, you might want to turn the music up a little louder. Although many Imbolc rituals can be performed outdoors (yes, even in February!), this one is really geared for indoors. An outdoor skyclad Imbolc ritual is only for the bravest and toughest among us! If you share a bedroom, that room is a good location choice as long as there is space for you to sit together on the floor.

Spread out the altar cloth. You can use a low table as an altar if you like, but this is a ritual that works well sitting on the floor (if you are physically able). Be sure that whatever surface you use is safe for candles. With a total of three candles and incense burning, a sturdy surface is important to keep your altar tools from tipping over. Setting your house on fire would not be a good way to show your love for one another! Place both white candles in their respective holders. Place one on the left side of the altar and the other on the right. Traditionally, the man's candle would go on the right and woman's on the left, but in modern magick you can alter that in any way you prefer. In same-sex relationships, the distinction between "male" and "female" sides of an altar might even be meaningless to you. The deities are more flexible about this sort of thing than most people, so adjust the altar to fit your particular circumstance. Simply decide who will be on which side of the altar, and lay out your tools accordingly. Using terms like "the person on the left side of the altar" may lack poetry but makes up for it with inclusiveness.

Next, place the red candle in the center of the altar cloth. If you are using essential oils, place a tiny amount of each into a small dish or bowl. Only a few drops of each scent are needed. Participants should place their oil next to the candle on their side of the altar cloth. If you are using incense sticks, participants should likewise place their incense next to the white candle that represents them. The empty chalice should be placed a few inches in front of the red candle. If you are using incense, the censer should be a few inches in front of the chalice. Finally, place the two small glasses on the altar, one on each side.

Before the ritual begins, light both of the white candles and partially fill both of the small glasses and place on either side of the altar. Ultimately, the liquids in the two small glasses will be combined and then consumed, so participants might want to keep that in mind when selecting a liquid. While you could put milk in one glass and vodka in the other, I can't imagine that would create something drinkable. If the vodka were replaced with chocolate syrup, that might have a more pleasant result. If you are uncertain about a choice of liquids, you can never go wrong with pure, clean water.

With the lights and music adjusted, the door secured, and the candles burning, you can begin the ritual. If you want to perform this ritual skyclad, disrobe just before you begin. Both participants should sit in front of the altar (on the south side if your altar is oriented to the north) facing one another. Sit any way that is comfortable for you. Before you begin, take a few moments to clear your minds. When you are ready to start, look into the eyes of your partner to ensure she or he is also ready to begin.

The person sitting on the right (east if you altar is oriented to north) begins. Remember that the words that follow are only generalized suggestions. You should try and make your words as specific, personal, and meaningful to your partner as possible.

I have loved you since my eyes first met yours.

What might have been an empty and hollow life
has been brought into the light of your love.

You have filled my soul and my heart—
I would be incomplete without you.

[Point to the white taper candle on the altar's right side]

This candle is the light you have brought into my life.

Your light forces away the shadows from my
mind and brings joy and security to my life.

The person on the left side responds:

I have loved you for just as long.

When you first touched my soul,
you set me alight with a bright flame.

You have filled my heart and my soul with
love beyond what I ever believed possible.

I didn't know how empty my life was until your
light filled that dark, empty space within me.

[Point to the white taper on the altar's left side]

This candle is the light you have brought into my life.

Your light has shown me love unlike
any I could have imagined.

Blending our lives has created a unique
flavor I could never have imagined.

Lift your glass from the left side of the altar and pour some liquid into the chalice.

The person on the right then responds:

Our life together is a flavor I never
could have imagined before.

Now I can't imagine living without it.

Lift your glass from the right side of the altar and pour some of your liquid into the chalice. You can allow the liquids to blend naturally or you could stir them together at this point. Each of you should insert the index finger of you dominant hand into the chalice and stir the liquid together. If you prefer to keep fingers out of your drink, use a wood craft stick or coffee stirrer. Overlap dominant hands on the stirrer and both stir the mixture together. Now both people say:

Two become one and the one empowers two.

Using both hands, both of you hold the chalice at eye level. As the person on the right takes a drink from the chalice, the person on the left should say:

Tonight, my spirit is yours and yours is mine.

As the liquids meld, so do our souls.

As the person on the left takes a drink, the person on the right repeats the same words. Return the chalice to the altar. If you have chosen to use oils in the ritual, both people should "dress" the candle with the oil from their side of the altar. It's important to remember that pure essential oils shouldn't be handled with bare skin. If you are using an essential oil in carrier oil, it may be safe to apply to the candle with your fingers. Otherwise, apply the oil with a small cloth.

If you have chosen to include incense in the ritual, both people should light the incense on their side of the altar using the candle on their side. Insert both sticks into your incense holder side by side. Once you have the red candle dressed or the incense burning in its censer, both say:

> *Two souls become one just as two scents become one.*
>
> *Two souls become one just as two flames become one.*

Join hands over the chalice (person on the right uses left hand, person on the left uses right hand). Each lift your candle with your free hand and together light the red candle using both candles. Return the candles to the altar. At this point you will have created some pretty intense energy that can be celebrated sexually or enjoyed as extraordinary time together.

When you are finished, extinguish the candles as discussed earlier in this book. If the incense is still burning, it should be allowed to burn out naturally if you will be in the room. Never leave incense, candles, or anything else burning when you are not in the room to ensure you will be around for many more Imbolcs to come.

Uncoiling the Dragon: A Group Ritual

Imbolc is a time when the earth is beginning to wake in preparation for spring, which is just around the corner. It is the time of the earth's "quickening," when new life and new ideas begin to stir. Imbolc is also a celebration of fire and light. The dragon is a symbol long associated with both ideas, and it is also associated with Brigid and Imbolc. This ritual awakens the sleepy spirit from its winter rest and gives life and energy to the ideas that are about to take form on the physical plane. Just as hibernating animals begin to stir in the last of the winter snow, the dragon that lives within the world (and inside each one of us) also awakens. The earth's dragon will walk with you until winter returns. At Imbolc it is ready to rise, stretch, and warm us from the inside out.

The focal point of the ritual is an altar draped with a yellow cloth representing the warming sun above us as well as the earth's hot core beneath us. Coiled around these givers of heat lies the dragon of the earth. Ritual participants will build their own replica of the dragon and not only awaken him but fly with him as he lights a candle for each person. The person nearest the altar will light a candle that will pass slowly up the spine of the dragon to his head. With his fire restored after his slumber, he will uncoil from his warm bed and offer his fire for each participant's goal for the coming warm days.

This ritual is intended for five or more people, but you can have fun trying it with fewer people if you'd like. Thirteen is a perfect number of people for this ritual but it can be easily adapted for much larger groups. While groups are often organized as covens, there are many times when rituals involve groups with less formal organization (for example, at a public ritual or part of a large festival). To cover all of those possibilities, let's use the terms "lead" to refer to the person at the head of the dragon and "anchor" to refer to the person at the end of the dragon's tail rather than the titles of High Priestess and High Priest. The anchor begins the chain of people who will form the dragon's body.

This ritual does not have to be performed within the confines of a magick circle. If your group normally works within a circle you can still perform the ritual if you remember that you may need one larger than you would normally cast. You need enough space for your entire group to hold hands and form a large circle. An altar table can serve as the center point for this ritual, and if you're going to do this outdoors, a small balefire could serve as the center point with an altar table adjacent to it.

You will need:

- An altar table in the center of the ritual area (optionally, adjacent to a balefire)

- A yellow altar cloth

- A white pillar candle

- A white taper candle

- A candleholder for the taper, one that can be easily passed from one person to another while the candle is burning. A candle lantern that has glass or metal mesh around the candle prevents accidental contact with the flame; these are perfect for this ritual.

- Dragon's blood incense and censer. Sticks or cones are the most convenient to use, but charcoal and pure dragon's blood resin will also work well. If you do not have access to natural dragon's blood incense (not "dipped" incense) you could use any natural incense. Tarragon burned on charcoal is a good substitute (*tarragon* means "little dragon").

- Additional candles and holders. Have each participant bring one personal candle (of any color or design) and an appropriate holder. If you are using a candle lantern, the "lead" (the "head" of the dragon) should select a taper candle for a personal candle.

The altar should be covered with the yellow cloth with the white pillar candle in the center, along with the incense and censer. Light the candle before you begin, and if you are using charcoal to burn your incense, that should also be lit in advance. A stick or cone of incense can be lit during the ritual or when the pillar candle is lit. The white taper candle should be lying on the table next to its holder or lantern.

As participants come into the ritual area, they should place their personal candles (already placed in the candleholder) on the altar table. When you are ready to get started, everyone should stand in a circle in the same order they will stand when the ritual begins (the lead and anchor people will stand next to each other to close the loop). Everyone will face the altar table and hold hands while extending into the largest circle that is comfortable for the space. Once the circle is formed, everyone can let go of one another's hands.

To begin building the dragon, the anchor will go to the altar, retrieve her candle and holder. She will then return to her place in the circle of people and place her candle into the holder where she had been standing. The anchor should then stand next to the altar (in front of the unlit taper candle) and face the white pillar candle. With the anchor in place, the dragon spirals out from the tail.

The person standing to the left of the anchor's empty spot in the circle will retrieve her candle and return it to take her place in the circle. She should then stand to the right of the anchor, also facing the white pillar candle.

One by one, each person will get her candle from the altar, put it in her place in the circle, and then join the others around the altar. As more people gather around the altar, remember that you are making a single spiral, not a series of circles. As the line of people wraps around the anchor, it should overlap and continue on as a single, unbroken line. Once in the spiral, everyone should face the altar. As people come up to get their candles, make a space for them to get through the spiral to reach the altar.

As you continue to add more people to your slumbering dragon, it will spiral out from the altar. If you could see it from above, it would appear as a counterclockwise spiral, but you will see that the dragon will emerge from it flying clockwise. Once the lead is in place the real fun begins. The "lead" is now the dragon's head and the "anchor" the tip of the dragon's tail. The lead should signal she is in place so the anchor can begin.

If you are using stick or cone incense, the anchor should first light the incense from the flame of the pillar candle. If using charcoal, add several pinches of incense to its surface. Then call the dragon into your ritual:

> *Great old dragon, guardian of earth's*
> *warmth, bringer of blessings, we call you in*
> *to the spiral we have made in your honor.*

The anchor should then light the taper candle on the altar from the pillar candle. If using a candle lantern, she will need to insert the candle and close the lantern. The anchor should loudly proclaim:

> *Great dragon, we offer you this flame from the*
> *heart of our altar to rekindle your sleeping fires.*

The group should answer with equal gusto:

Great dragon, awaken!

Using great caution, the anchor should pick up the candle and pass it to the person on her right, saying, "Blessings of the flame." Continue passing the candleholder or lantern to the right with the blessing offered each time. Take care not to burn anyone if you are using an open flame. When the candle has been handed to the lead, that person then becomes the head of the dragon, saying:

We call upon you, great old dragon, to take the flame we offer, that you may awaken from the slumber of the dark days and bless us as we prepare for the fertile days that are fast approaching.

The group should then chant "Awake! Awake! AWAKE!"

Holding the candleholder or lantern high, the lead calls, "The dragon has awakened and is ready to fly!"

Now it's time for the dragon to fly! The dragon's head turns 180 degrees, and with candleholder or lantern held at the front of the line, begins to move clockwise behind the rest of the dragon. As the head moves behind each participant, that person will also turn and join the flying dragon.

Continue uncoiling the dragon until the anchor has joined the flight. Once the anchor is moving around the circle with everyone else, the lead will continue around until reaching her candle sitting at the edge of the circle.

As the lead approaches that stopping point, the entire dragon should be slowed. As the dragon ends his flight, participants should be standing near their candle. The dragon's flight is complete once all participants are standing at their own candles.

With everyone standing at their candles, the lead should remove the burning taper if a candle lantern was used. The lead should proclaim:

The dragon is awake and shall share the
good fortune of his warming fire with us all.

She should then kneel and use the taper to light her personal candle. Once the lead's candle is burning, she should pass the burning taper clockwise. Everyone will light their candles in the same way, passing the burning taper clockwise. When the anchor's candle is burning, the burning taper should be handed back to the lead, who will say:

We celebrate the awakening of the dragon
who heralds the approaching spring.

The dragon has given flame to our plans for the
spring and has given a blessing to each of us.

We thank you Great Old Dragon and hope
that you will grant us the strength of your
flame until the dark days return again.

We thank you for joining us and sharing your warmth.

From a tiny flame, great fires can grow.

The participants are welcome, even in a rowdy fashion, to bid farewell and give their thanks to the dragon of the earth. Everyone can enjoy the energy of the flight as their candles burn. If you share a feast with your group as part of your rituals, this is a great time to do that. Optionally, personal candles can be extinguished (keeping in mind the guidelines in "New Ways") at any time and the participants can go their own ways. If you work within a magick circle, remember to properly banish the circle before any candles are extinguished.

Imbolc is a time when we can safely discard the things that are holding us back. It's a time to embrace change. We can reflect on what was and what could have been. Imbolc is also a time of hope, and it is perfect for cleaning and preparing for the warmer days ahead. However, we are also required to discard and let go of whatever restrains us; new paths and ideas await us. This quiet sabbat might arrive in your neighborhood when there is still a thick blanket of snow on the ground, or weeks after the daffodils have burst forth with the colors of spring. Regardless of the weather around you, you can find ways to embrace and celebrate this sabbat's subtle nature.

CORRESPONDENCES
FOR
IMBOLC

...e beginnings, birth, renewal, rejuvenation, balance, fertility, change, strength, vernal equinox, sun enters Aries, Libra in the Sou... Green Man, Amalthea, Aphrodite, Blodeuwedd, Eostre, Eos...a, Flora, Freya, Gaia, Guinevere, Persephone, Libera, Ne... ...enpet, Umaj, Vila, Aengus MacOg, Cernunnos, Herma, The ...Kama, Mabon Osiris, Pan, Thor, abundance, growth, health, cr...al healing, patience understanding virtue, spring, honor, contentm... ...chic abilities, spiritual truth, intuition, receptivity, love, inner se... ...provement, spiritual awareness, purification, childhood, innocence ...lity, creativity, communication, concentration, divination, harmo... ...abilities, prosperity, attraction, blessings, happiness, luck, money ...ty, guidance, visions, insight, family, wishes, celebrating life cyc... ...riendship, courage, attracts love, honesty, good health, emotions, ..., improvement, influence, motivation, peace, rebirth, self preserva... ...minine power, freedom, optimism, new beginnings, vernal equinox ...creation, sun, apple blossom, columbine, crocus, daffodil, daisy ...isy, honeysuckle, jasmine, jonquil, lilac, narcissus, orange blossom ...mrose, rose, the fool, the magician, the priestess, justice, the sta... ...ts gathering growth abundance eggs seeds honey dill orange...

Spiritual Focus and Key Words
Beginnings
preparation
patience
awakening
thrift
newness/renewal
"child-like delight in all things" (Starhawk)
innocence
change
emergence from sleep/hibernation
cleansing
sprouting seeds
fertility
transitions

Magical Focus and Suggested Workings

Cleansing
protection
divination
birth/rebirth
transformation
youth
well-being
emergence
awakenings

Astrological Timing and Associated Planets

Astronomical midpoint between the winter solstice and the vernal equinox; Sun at 15° of Aquarius in Northern Hemisphere, Sun at 15° of Leo in Southern Hemisphere. Some Pagans celebrate Imbolc on the astronomical date; others stick to February 2 out of tradition.

Archetypes

FEMALE
The Goddess transforming from
    Crone to Maiden
the Goddess in the form of young
    mother tending to her growing child

MALE

God in the form of a child
  exploring the world
the innocence of the masculine

Deities and Heroes

GODDESSES

Brigid (Irish)

Aphrodite / Venus (Greco-Roman)

Diana (Etruscan / Roman)

Arianrhod (Welsh)

Artio (Swiss)

Athena (Greek)

Danu (Irish)

Gaia (Greek)

Inanna (Hausa / West Africa)

Juno (Roman)

Selene (Greek)

Vesta (Roman)

Selu (Cherokee)

Gods

Februus (Roman)

Bragi (Norse)

Cupid (Roman)

Dian Cecht (Irish)

Dumuzi (Sumarian)

Eros (Greek)

Colors

Light Green: Abundance, growth, fertility,
   health, calming, new beginnings, prosperity

Pink: Harmony, tenderness, affection, love, spiritual
   healing, virtue, spring, honor, contentment

White: Cleansing, peace, protection, healing, truth,
   divination, purification, childhood, innocence

Yellow: Joy, vitality, creativity, communication,
   the sun, planning, psychic ability, attraction

Herbs

Angelica: Balance, new beginnings, consecration,
   insight, purification, stability, success

Basil: Clarity, divination, love, money,
   protection, strength, success

Blackberry/Bramble: Growth, attachments, fertility,
   intuition, prosperity, protection, purification

Cinnamon: Balance, blessings, courage, protection, purification, strength, success

Grain: Protection, abundance, fertility, community, balance, birth/rebirth, blessing

Reed: Action, awareness, confidence, growth, healing, inspiration, protection, unity

Wormwood: Banishing, divination/dream work, forgiveness, overcoming obstacles, purification

Trees

Blackthorn: Banishing, guidance, obstacles, protection, strength, magick

Cedar: Affection, balance, calm, clarity, community, blessing, growth, fertility, peace, purification, success

Rowan: Authority, blessings, challenges, devotion, divination, enchantment, fertility, forgiveness, inspiration

Sycamore: Abundance, communication, determination, harmony, learning, love, obstacles, protection, stability, wisdom

Flowers

Crocus: Attract love, visions, sobriety, and rebirth

Daffodil: Calm, fairies, fertility, love, perseverance, magick, wishing

Crystals and Stones

Amethyst: Dreams, healing, courage, happiness, balance, beginnings, change, divination, growth, rebirth, transformation

Turquoise: Attraction, balance, clarity, compassion, courage, healing, improvement, inner strength, wisdom

Metals

Antimony: Protection, shielding, energy, and strength

Brass: Balance, reversal, security, and solar energies

Gold: Authority, power, success, wisdom, light/ illumination, purification, strength, success

Animals, Totems, and Mythical Creatures

Cow: Abundance, comfort, nourishment, pregnancy/ childbirth, love, home, and warmth; the cow is one of the symbols of the goddess Brigid.

Dragon: Balance, challenges, courage, creativity, dignity, enlightenment, guardian, wisdom, and power; the dragon is closely tied to this time of year and to the goddess Bridgid.

Groundhog: Beginnings, community, cycles, family, rebirth, divination, earth energies; if the groundhog sees its shadow on Imbolc it means that spring will come late.

Lark: A lark singing on Imbolc means an early spring

Robin: Change, growth, omens, wishes; the robin is often the first sign of spring. Shows the end of the cold winter and announces the coming of the sun and warmer days.

Sheep: Abundance, balance, beginnings, nurturing, security, support; "Imbolc" refers to the first lactation of sheep; an early sign spring is coming.

Snake: Change, cunning, cycles, rebirth, wisdom, enchantment; as the snake is reborn after shedding skin, the snake represents changes and new beginnings. The snake is also closely associated with the goddess Brigid.

Swan: Awakening, beauty, grace, innocence, sleep, transformation, trust. The swan has long been a symbol of change and transformation, even representing the transition between life and death.

Scents for Oils, Incense, Potpourri, or Just Floating in the Air

Cedar

peppermint

styrax

basil

cinnamon

Tarot Keys

Death

the Empress

the Star

Symbols and Tools

Brid's Cross / Brighid's Cross

corn dollies

Brid's bed

candles

Saint Brighid

Saint Mary

the cauldron

broom / besom

whistle

Foods

Dried fruits

grains

potatoes

cornmeal

dried / salted meats

cheese

pickled or canned foods

nuts

eggs

Drinks

All dairy products
ale
mead
cider

Activities and Traditions of Practice

Making a corn dolly or Brigid's Cross
candle making and/or blessing
making fortune cookies
dedicate new magickal tools
blessing of animals
blessing of new projects
divination
fireworks

Acts of Service

Clear snow/ice from public walkways
gather blankets for the needy
clear and prepare a community garden or flower bed for
    planting; clean the home of a physically limited person

Alternate Names for Imbolc in other Pagan Traditions

Imbolc or Imbolg (Gaelic, "in the belly,"
   referring to the ewes' first milk of the year)

Oimelc (Saxon, "ewe's milk")

Feast of Brighid

Lá Fhéile Bríde (Irish)

Laa'l Breeshey (Manx)

Feast of Mary of the Candles (Welsh)

Holidays or Traditions Occurring During
Imbolc in the Northern Hemisphere

RELIGIOUS

Feast Day of Saint Brigit of Kildare (Catholic, February 1)

Presentation of Jesus at the Temple or Candlemas (Christian,
   February 2, also called "Feast of the Purification of the
   Virgin," and "the Meeting of the Lord")

The Feast of St. Valentine (February 14)

Lupercalia / Pan's Day (February 15)

Milk / Nursing Moon (varies but usually during Imbolc)

Pre-Lenten festivals and start of Lent (Catholic,
   moveable dates; between February 4 and March 10)

Parinirvana / Nirvana Day (Mahayana
   Buddhist, February 8 or Feb. 15)

Groundhog Day (February 2)

Valentine's Day (February 14)

Chinese New Year (varies)

Mardi Gras (varies)

Holidays or Traditions Occurring During Imbolc in the Southern Hemisphere

RELIGIOUS

Festival of the Dryads (Grecian, August 1–3)

Nemoralia (Roman, August 13–15)

Tisha B'Av (Jewish, July or August, variable
   dates according to the lunar calendar)

Assumption Day (Christian, August 15)

SECULAR

Picnic Day (Autralia's Northern
   Territory, first Monday of August)

National Women's Day (South Africa, August 9)

Various independence days in South America: July 9,
   Argentina; July 28, Peru; August 6, Bolivia;
   August 10, Ecuador; Aug. 25: Uruguay; July 24,
Birth of Simon Bolivar, liberator of Venezuela,
   Colombia, Ecuador, Peru, and Bolivia,
Heroes' Day (various African countries, July / August)
Farmers' Day (various African countries, July / August)

FURTHER
READING

If you'd like to delve deeper into the topics in this book, there are
plenty of great places to turn for more information. One good
place to look for additional reading is the bibliography, and I've
also included a list to get you started. What is presented here
only scratches the surface of the information available, but these
books are great gateways to learn even more.

If ritual practices interest you, there are many wonderful books that more deeply explore not only how rituals and
magickal tools are used but how they are created. One of the
most popular books of all time on this topic is Scott Cunningham's amazing little book *Wicca: A Guide for the Solitary Practitioner*

(Llewellyn, 1988). For more rituals and the stories behind them, you might enjoy Patricia Montley's *In Nature's Honor: Myths and Rituals Celebrating the Earth* (Skinner House, 2005). For a more encyclopedic view of rituals tools and their use, my book *The Magick Toolbox: The Ultimate Compendium for Choosing and Using Ritual Implements and Magickal Tools* (Weiser, 2004) is a good starting place for learning basic and advanced techniques as well as making your own tools.

If divination interests you, *Cunningham's Divination for Beginners: Reading the Past, Present & Future* (Llewellyn, 2003) is a fantastic starting place. P. Scott Hollander's *Tarot for Beginners: An Easy Guide to Understanding & Interpreting the Tarot* (Llewellyn, 1995) will introduce you to divination through the tarot. If astrology holds your interest, *Magickal Astrology: Understanding Your Place in the Cosmos* (Career Press, 2008) by Skye Alexander is a good starting place.

If the goddess Brigid interests you, there are many books to give you a deeper look into one of the central deities of Celtic belief. Michelle Skye's *Goddess Alive: Inviting Celtic & Norse Goddess Into Your Life* (Llewellyn, 2007), *Celtic Goddess: Warriors, Virgins and Mothers* by Miranda Green (George Braziller, 1995), and Alexei Kondratiev's *The Apple Branch: A Path to Celtic Ritual* (Citadel, 2003) can all guide you along Brigid's sacred path.

If the celebration of Neopagan sabbats interests you, the first place to look would be the other books in this series. Like this one, each book explores a different sabbat in ancient as well as modern times. The books in this series are an excellent introduction to the meaning and practices around all eight sabbats.

Many books explore all the sabbats in a single volume. Although books of this type won't provide the depth of information that the individual books of this series do, they do illustrate how the wheel of the year brings all the sabbats together. Edain McCoy's *The Sabbats: A New Approach to Living the Old Ways* (Llewellyn, 1998) and *Celebrating the Seasons of Life: Samhain to Ostara* by Ashleen O'Gaea (Career Press, 2009) can give you that "big picture" view of the sabbats and their relationships. I also have to mention Ellen Dugan's *Seasons of Witchery: Celebrating the Sabbats with the Garden Witch* (Llewellyn, 2012), which is a new favorite of mine.

If the lives of ancient peoples and their beliefs interest you, check out any books by Joseph Campbell, such as *The Power of Myth* (Anchor, 1991) for a classic look. For a different perspective, try *Goddess: Myths of the Female Divine* by David Leeming and Jake Page (Oxford University Press, 1994). For a truly academic look, but written by renowned Pagan professor Dr. Ronald Hutton, read *The Pagan Religions of the Ancient British Isles: Their Nature and Legacy* (Wiley-Blackwell, 1993).

If history interests you, there are some excellent books about the history of the Neopagan movement, and some foundational books that actually form that history available.

Starhawk's *The Spiral Dance: A Rebirth of the Ancient Religion of the Great Goddess* (HarperOne, 1979) is one of the foundational texts of modern Paganism. Margot Adler's *Drawing Down the Moon: Witches, Druids, Goddess-Worshippers, and Other Pagans in America* (Viking Press, 1979) documents the early history of the Neopagan movement in America. Dr. Hutton has written on this topic as well in his book *The Triumph of the Moon: A History of Modern Pagan Witchcraft* (Oxford, 2001).

I can't begin to list all of the many wonderful books about gardening currently in print, but if you are new to gardening and interested in learning, you might start with *The New Western Garden Book: The Ultimate Gardening Guide* (Oxmoor House, 2012) or *Trowel and Error: Over 700 Tips, Remedies and Shortcuts for the Gardener* (Workman Publishing Company, 2002). Gardening is an industry unto itself, and the books on the topic are seemingly endless. These books serve new and seasoned gardeners alike, and they will help you decide what areas to study next.

There are some wonderful books out there about "crafting for the Craft." *Bewitching Cross Stitch* by Joan Elliott (David & Charles, 2008) is one of many books that let your hands create fun craft items. One of my all-time favorite crafting books is Scott Cunningham and David Harrington's *Spell Crafts: Creating Magical Objects* (Llewellyn, 1994). Just reading that book has often inspired me to create original craft items in addition to the projects in the book. Another craft that has been written about exhaustively is cooking. I won't pretend to steer you through the enormous world of books about cooking, but if Craft cooking interests you, look for a copy of Cait Johnson's *Witch in the Kitchen: Magical Cooking for All Seasons* (Destiny Books, 2001). If you want to learn all the mechanical details of every type of cooking imaginable, I would suggest the beloved ancient tome of American cooking, *The Joy of Cooking* by Irma Rombauer and Marion Rombauer Becker, in its many, many editions (first published by Scribner, 1931).

BIBLIOGRAPHY

Alexander, Skye. *Magickal Astrology: Understanding Your Place in the Cosmos*. Franklin Lakes, NJ: New Page Books, 2008.

Buckland, Raymond. *The Witch Book: The Encyclopedia of Witchcraft, Wicca, and Neo-paganism*. Detroit: Visible Ink, 2002.

"Chinese Spring Festival 2015: Tradition, History, Day-By-Day Guide," available from www.chinahighlights.com /travelguide/special-report/chinese-new-year; accessed 20 December 2014.

"Commercial Sheep Production," available from
www.aces.nmsu.edu/sheep/management_systems
/commercial_prod.html; accessed 5 December 2014.

Cunningham, Scott. *The Complete Book Of Incense, Oils &
Brews*. St. Paul, MN: Llewellyn Publications, 1989.

———. *Cunningham's Encyclopedia Of Crystal, Gem & Metal
Magic*. St. Paul, MN: Llewellyn Publications, 1987.

———. *Cunningham's Encyclopedia Of Magical
Herbs*. St. Paul, MN: Llewellyn Publications, 1985.

———. *Magical Herbalism*. St. Paul, MN: Llewellyn
Publications, 1998.

———. *Wicca: A Guide for the Solitary Practitioner*.
St. Paul, MN: Llewellyn Publications, 1988.

Ferguson, Anna-Marie. *A Keeper of Words*.
St. Paul, MN: Llewellyn Publications, 1995.

Gimenez, Diego. "Reproductive Management of Sheep
and Goats," available from aces.edu/pubs/docs
/A/ANR-1316/ANR-1316.pdf; accessed 19
December 2014.

"Groundhog Day History," available from www.groundhog
.org/groundhog-day/history/; accessed 24 July 2014.

Hinshaw, Annette. *Earth Time, Moon Time.*
St. Paul, MN: Llewellyn Publications, 1999.

Hollander, P. Scott. *Tarot for Beginners.*
St. Paul, MN: Llewellyn Publications, 1995.

Illes, Judika. *The Element Encyclopedia of Witchcraft.*
Hammersmith, London: HarperElement, 2005.

K, Azreal Arynn & K, Amber. *Candlemas: Feast of
Flames.* St. Paul, MN: Llewellyn Publications, 2001.

Kynes, Sandra. *Llewellyn's Complete Books of Correspondences.*
St. Paul, MN: Llewellyn Publications, 2013.

Leeming, David and Page, Jake. *Goddess: Myths of the Female
Divine.* New York: Oxford University Press, 1994.

Luenn, Nancy. *Celebrations of Light.* New York:
Atheneum Books for Young Readers, 1998.

McCoy, Edain. *The Sabbats: A New Approach to Living the
Old Ways.* St. Paul, MN: Llewellyn Publications, 1998.

Merrill, William and Ives Goddard. "Essays in Honor of
William Curtis Sturtevant," *Smithsonian Contributions to
Anthropology 44.* Washington, DC: Smithsonian Institution
Press, 2002.

Montley, Patricia. *In Nature's Honor: Myths and Rituals Celebrating
the Earth.* Boston: Skinner House Books, 2005.

Morgan, Ffiona. *Wild Witches Don't Get The Blues.* Rio Nido, CA: Daughters of the Moon Publishing, 1991.

Neal, Carl F. *Incense: Crafting and Use of Magickal Scents.* St. Paul, MN: Llewellyn Publications, 2003.

O'Gaea, Ashleen. *Celebrating the Seasons of Life: Samhain to Ostara.* Franklin Lakes, NJ: New Page Books, 2009.

Owen, Lara. "Imbolc: The Quickening of the Year," available from www.patheos.com/blogs/planetaryenergies/2013/02/imbolc-the-quickening-of-the-year; accessed 22 July 2014.

"Reproduction in the ewe," available from www.sheep101.info/201/ewerepro.html; accessed 13 December 2014.

"Sheep Gestation Table Lambing Date Calculator," available from www.tvsp.org/gestation.html; accessed 13 December 2014.

Skye, Michelle. *Goddess Alive: Inviting Celtic & Norse Goddess Into Your Life.* Woodbury, MN: Llewellyn Publications, 2007.

Starhawk. *The Spiral Dance: A Rebirth of the Ancient Religion of the Great Goddess.* San Francisco: HarperSanFrancisco, 1979.

Thompson, Sue Ellen. *Holiday Symbols and Customs: Third Edition.* Detroit: Omnigraphics, Inc., 2003.

Walter, Philippe. *Christianity: The Origins of a Pagan Religion.* Rochester, VT: Inner Traditions, 2006.

Wigington, Patti. "Groundhog Day," available from Paganwiccan.about.com/od/imbolcfebruary2/p/GroundhogDay.htm; accessed 24 July 2014.

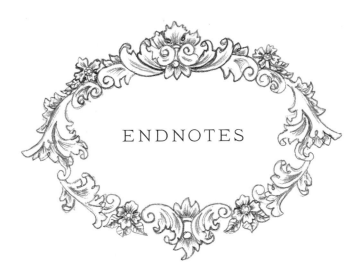

ENDNOTES

1. Gimenez, Diego. "Reproductive Management of Sheep and Goats," available from www.aces.edu/pubs /docs/A/ANR-1316/ANR-1316.pdf.

2. "Reproduction in the ewe," available from www .sheep101.info/201/ewerepro.html; "Commercial Sheep Production," available from www.aces.nmsu .edu/sheep/management_systems/commercial _prod.html; "Sheep Gestation Table Lambing Date Calculator," available from www.tvsp.org/gestation.html.

3. "Venerable Brigid (Bridget) of Ireland," available from oca.org/saints/lives/2000/02/01/100406-venerable -brigid-bridget-of-ireland.

4. *The Element Encyclopedia of Witchcraft*, 300.

5. Ibid.

6. *The Witch Book: The Encyclopedia of Witchcraft, Wicca, and Neo-paganism*, 99.

7. *Encyclopedia of Spirits*, 866–867.

8. "Chinese Spring Festival 2015: Tradition, History, Day-By-Day Guide" available from www.chinahighlights .com/travelguide/special-report/chinese-new-year

9. *Holidays, Symbols, and Customs*, 82–83.

10. *Candlemas: Feast of Flames*, 16.

INDEX

About the Author

Carl leaned towards a Pagan path from early childhood but did not find his feet firmly on that path until having tried a variety of other spiritualities along the way. In 1995 he began to attend Pagan festivals and openly display his long-held beliefs. The warmth and sincerity of the Pagan Community was exactly what he'd been trying to find.

Although he spent time practicing group magick and still has ties to a coven, Carl has long been a Solitary Pagan. His efforts to build the Pagan Community may not seem like a typical priority for Solitaries, but he believes this duality is the future of Paganism. Carl has long been a student of both nature and energy, two building blocks of modern Paganism. As a historian, he enjoys researching and teaching about how ancient beliefs can be blended into a modern spirituality. Carl began teaching at Pagan events and festivals in the late 1990s and continues to teach to this day. While best known for his work on incense and incense making, he has long taught about making and using ritual tools, Guardians and the building of community, and other topics that bring life to a full Pagan life.

Carl currently lives with his family in Western Oregon. He holds a Bachelor's degree in both History and Sociology.

GET MORE AT **LLEWELLYN.COM**

Visit us online to browse hundreds of our books and decks, plus sign up to receive our e-newsletters and exclusive online offers.

- • **Free tarot readings • Spell-a-Day • Moon phases**
- • **Recipes, spells, and tips • Blogs • Encyclopedia**
- • **Author interviews, articles, and upcoming events**

GET SOCIAL WITH **LLEWELLYN**

Find us on   **@LlewellynBooks**

www.Facebook.com/LlewellynBooks

GET BOOKS AT **LLEWELLYN**

LLEWELLYN ORDERING INFORMATION

 Order online: Visit our website at www.llewellyn.com to select your books and place an order on our secure server.

Order by phone:
- • Call toll free within the US at 1-877-NEW-WRLD (1-877-639-9753)
- • We accept VISA, MasterCard, American Express, and Discover.

Order by mail:
Send the full price of your order (MN residents add 6.875% sales tax) in US funds plus postage and handling to: Llewellyn Worldwide, 2143 Wooddale Drive, Woodbury, MN 55125-2989

POSTAGE AND HANDLING

STANDARD (US): (Please allow 12 business days)
$30.00 and under, add $6.00.
$30.01 and over, FREE SHIPPING.

CANADA:
We cannot ship to Canada. Please shop your local bookstore or Amazon Canada.

INTERNATIONAL:
Customers pay the actual shipping cost to the final destination, which includes tracking information.

Visit us online for more shipping options.
Prices subject to change.

FREE CATALOG!

To order, call 1-877-NEW-WRLD ext. 8236 or visit our website

Don't forget to check out
all eight books in the
Llewellyn Sabbat Essentials Series:

. . . .

Imbolc

Yule

Samhain

Mabon

Lughnasadh

Midsummer

Beltane

Ostara

. . . .

Read on for more information
on these books, as well as others!